MACMILLAN MODERN

THEATRE FOR THE YOUNG

Alan England

Former Lecturer in Drama

University of Sheffield Division of Education

MACMILLAN

First published 1990

Published by
MACMILLAN EDUCATION LTD
Houndmills, Basingstoke, Hampshire RG21 2XS
and London
Companies and representatives
throughout the world

Printed in Hong Kong

British Library Cataloguing in Publication Data
England, Alan
Theatre for the young. — (Macmillan modern
dramatists)
1. Great Britain. Theatre for young persons
I. Title
792′.0226′0941
ISBN 0–333–35082–0 (hc)
ISBN 0–333–35083–9 (pbk)

Contents

List of Illustrations

Editors' Preface

The *Modern Dramatists* is an international series of introductions to major and significant nineteenth- and twentieth-century dramatists, movements and new forms of drama in Europe, Great Britain, America and new nations such as Nigeria and Trinidad. Besides new studies of great and influential dramatists of the past, the series includes volumes on contemporary authors, recent trends in the theatre and on many dramatists, such as writers of farce, who have created theatre 'classics' while being neglected by literary criticism. The volumes in the series devoted to individual dramatists include a biography, a survey of the plays, and detailed analysis of the most significant plays, along with discussion, where relevant, of the political, social, historical and theatrical context. The authors of the volumes, who are involved with theatre as playwrights, directors, actors, teachers and critics, are concerned with the plays as theatre and discuss such matters as performance, character interpretation and staging, along with themes and contexts.

BRUCE KING
ADELE KING

Acknowledgements

I should like to thank the University of Sheffield Research Fund, the British Academy and the British Council for their financial assistance; my wife Mary and Joy Gargett for attending dozens of theatrical performances with me and giving me the benefit of their own acute observations; and the many personnel working in Young People's Theatre for the generous gifts of their time and courtesy in allowing themselves to be interviewed.

To the memory of my parents

1
Definitions and Principles

The subject of this book is theatre created specifically with young audiences in mind, for the most part in Great Britain but with some comparative references to what has gone on and what is going on in the United States of America and in East Germany. For practical reasons, it will be limited to theatre which expresses itself in plays and plays performed by human actors, and it will not attempt to encompass and thereby possibly do scant justice to puppetry and dance. It will also concentrate on plays produced by professional or amateur companies. This is in no way to undervalue the work of Youth Theatres. Youth Theatre is defined by the Standing Conference of Young People's Theatre (SCYPT) as 'theatre *done by young people themselves*, usually led by a teacher or under the auspices of a Young People's Company'. I acknowledge the fact that such work can sometimes issue in an artistic statement of high quality but its value resides at least partly in the benefit it affords to the participants and, in the last analysis, this takes priority. It is exclusively with theatre for young people as an art form and as practised by adults that the book will deal.

Thus, if I may invoke the help of SCYPT still further, my area of concern may embrace what they classify as Children's Theatre, that is 'work done by professional actors whose *primary aim* is to *entertain* children in the theatre form, or to increase their appreciation of Theatre as an art form'; and Young People's Theatre (YPT) 'the umbrella heading for *all* work done by *professional actors* for young people and children with an *educational purpose*'. SCYPT subdivides YPT into Educational Theatre, defined as 'theatre done by professional actors in youth clubs or similar venues. Its primary aim, like Theatre in Education is *educational*, but generally restricted to a play for a large number of young people (up to 200)'; and Theatre in Education (TIE), defined as 'work done by professional actor/teachers in a school context. Its primary aim is *to use* theatre and drama for educational purposes, i.e. to teach about something other than Theatre or theatre skills.'[1] TIE may include a play as part of its programme, though, whatever its main preoccupation.

The published scripts of plays for young people constitute a growing body of literature. Not all performances are based on or issue from a script, however, and, while trying to describe, account for and comment on 'trends', I have had to rely for evidence not merely on those scripts which are accessible to my reader, but on my own accounts, albeit as graphic as I can make them, of fleeting events at which, in all probability, the reader did not assist. But if, as I would argue, the play is the performance, all relevant 'evidence' is ultimately human action and the words on the page have to be judged in the light at least of their intended use. Each time even the printed play is performed, something unique and unrepeatable occurs. The theatrical event unfolds in time and space and works in terms not only of words but of gesture and sign. A number of people contribute towards its impact; besides the writer, there are 'stage artists' such as actor, director and designer. It is also an encounter between performers and audience and it is the interaction of these that determines its meaning. In investigating its nature, one must take into account the kind of company, where it originates and the company's intentions and assumptions. The physical and social setting, where the event takes place, the time of day and the duration of the event will also affect the way the performance is received and interpreted.

John Russell Brown makes out a strong case for 'considered reviewing' as the most appropriate method of study:

> Occasionally a critic can write about a single production twice or even three times as it moves from one theatre to another. But if he could see it many times, keeping touch with first impressions, and so compare one night's performance with another, and relate every detail of the production to every detail of the published text and, perhaps, to records of other productions; if he could assess an actor's performance in the light of his career as a whole, and compare the director's achievement with the designer's or the chief actor's; and if this critic had time to consider what the journalistic re-viewers have said and what the production has achieved in his own consciousness and to relate this to his personal views about man, society and life and to the views of

> others – then the critic might have found a full and careful way to study and criticise one theatrical experience.[2]

He adds that, as far as he knows, this recipe has never been followed and, so formidable are its demands, I certainly would not claim to have done so myself. But I have tried to proceed in the spirit of it and have tried to take account of individual ingredients. As well as my observations of effects, I have interviewed directors, actors and writers and have experience of my own as director, actor and writer of plays for the young to call upon.

The playwright (be he writer or deviser) must be attempting to find imaginative expression for his intuitions about the 'truth' of human motivation, behaviour and relationships but he will be discovering as he creates.[3] When the play is presented, it will enable both the audience and the actors to make further discoveries for themselves. As Martin Esslin puts it: 'All fiction, drama included, is true, if not in the facts about the external circumstances outlined in the story and the characters, all the more so in the insights through the characters into the author's mind and through that into the way we all think and feel.'[4] A good play will have its being somewhere between the artists and the audience and this implies that the audience will be allowed a degree of autonomy. To quote Martin Esslin again: 'The author, the director, the actors may have furnished us with clues to aid our interpretation, but that, in the last resort, must remain our own.'[5]

Does a children's play qualify as 'art'? Is it to be judged by these exacting standards? Theatre at any level must take into account what it gauges to be the character of its intended audience if it is to connect at all. But what distinguishes theatre for young people is the fact that it consciously addresses itself to the immature. Its purveyors are often tempted to make assumptions about the developmental needs and capabilities of the recipients. While admitting that individual differences may make generalisations hazardous, Moses Goldberg, the American academic, proceeds, undaunted, to propose that plays and performances should be fashioned, both in content and artistic sophistication, to match the stages of a child's psychological growth.[6] He divides the life of a child into four phases. Children under seven are active, curious, idealistic, optimistic, use other children merely as catalysts in their playing, enjoy trying out roles in recognisable settings, and have short attention spans. The theatre they need is visual, participatory; its favourite subjects fantasy creatures and animals. Children from seven to nine are preoccupied with rules and roles. Social mores become important and 'fairness' is at a premium. They like the 'good' and 'bad' clearly defined and distinguished and are strongly involved with stereotypes. Animals they still love, but myths, fairy-tales, mysteries and tales of foreign lands enter the arena. As this child is starting to choose the values he needs, theatre should offer a wide range of experiences and the more detached 'fourth wall' theatre should join participatory theatre in the repertoire. Children from ten to thirteen do not merely try out roles but examine them in order to make choices (Goldberg instances the case of Huckleberry Finn). Individuals count for more than right and wrong and social recognition is what matters now. Children of this age worship heroes, admire physical prowess. Boys love adventure, girls romance. Both need to be reassured that other people have the same weaknesses as they do and manage to survive. Young people of fourteen to eighteen also need recognition but also need to accept the limitations of being human. The choices with which they are now faced may be between different kinds of good and different kinds of evil. Actions can be both good and bad. 'Great analytical plays' are now appropriate, which show people making individual choices and which stimulate the formation of concepts. The big questions raised should be about the human condition itself.

A leading international figure in this field, Brian Way, also believes that theatre for youngsters should take account of the developmental stage of its audience. He, too, observes the needs of young children to 'play' and acknowledges the shortness of their attention span. The kind of theatre he favours is participatory theatre and he distinguishes three kinds of participation: spontaneous, stimulated and directed. In spontaneous participation, children are so emotionally involved that they bombard the actors with advice; in stimulated participation actors provoke the audience by word or deed to make suggestions or (for example) clean their teeth along with the character. In directed participation the help of the audience is actively sought in making decisions which will move the play forward. For young children (up to nine years of age), Way recommends that the audience remain in their seats; for children from nine to twelve, some of the audience might join the actors on the stage to enact them a journey, say; teenagers are ready for 'conscious theatre' and can be rehearsed for participation in crowd scenes.

Along with theories about what should constitute the appropriate content and form of plays for young people go theories about performances. Acting, for instance, should show, in Goldberg's view, a 'respect' for the audience. For children of all ages, Brian Way prefers a kind of acting based on the theory and practice of Stanislavsky, the principal requirements being 'absorption' and 'sincerity'. Other practitioners will instance 'patience' as being the prime virtue of the children's actor, or a clear and obvious 'out-front' style of presentation. For issue-based plays, the actor may be required to have an understanding of the themes of the piece as a whole, so that the 'problem' may be posed with true conviction.[7] There are conflicting theories about what kind of setting is best for children's theatre, from the shape of the auditorium to the realism of the scenery and props.

Those who write, select or commission plays for the young probably work mainly from observation and experience rather than from psychological or aesthetic speculation. However, the mere fact of attempting self-consciously to gauge and cater for a putative level of response has its dangers, and theatre for the young is notoriously prey to them. One is the danger of patronising. An Arts Council working party[8] found that a large percentage of plays it reported upon seriously underestimated their audiences. In an article in the *Guardian*, Michael Billington both agrees that this is so and deplores it.

> I begin to doubt the whole notion of a special ghetto area called 'Children's Theatre'. That belongs to a fast-fading, stratified culture in which serious things were for grown ups, and children, supposedly innocent of the world, had to be fed an anodyne substitute devoid of sex, violence, death and harsh reality. If you relied on the British Theatre solely for your information

about children, you would assume that they loved only furry animals, fairy tales, glove puppets, gingerbread men, dwarfs, giants and audience participation.

To Billington, 'the best theatre is that which adults and children can enjoy simultaneously'. Television has blurred the distinction between children and adults in so far as they share and enjoy the same programmes. 'They've heard of the pill, cocaine, muggings, unemployment, race-riots and Ulster.'[9]

The reference to 'gingerbread men' is a sideswipe at David Wood, dubbed by British journalists 'our national children's playwright', whose play *The Gingerbread Man* now appears regularly and ubiquitously at Christmas. Wood is an articulate and unashamed proponent of giving children what they want, and what they primarily want, according to him, is 'entertainment'. As he says in a letter to a friend of mine: 'I believe I am an entertainer rather than an educator. Theatre should be about entertainment; if that element is there, all the other elements like "message", "theme" or "moral" are possible, and sometimes, though not always, desirable.' 'Entertainment' means, for him, a 'magical experience' which is best engineered in a theatre boasting elaborate technical equipment. 'Lighting, scenery and costumes can all be used in the school hall, yet no-one can deny they may be more profitably employed in a theatre, offering all the old fashioned magic it has become fashionable to knock.'[10] The limitations of 'entertainment' have been well defined by Collingwood:

> If an artifact is designed to stimulate a certain emotion and if this emotion is intended not for discharge into the occupations of ordinary life, but for enjoyment as

> something of value in itself, the function of the artifact is to amuse or entertain . . . amusement is not useful but only enjoyable because there is a watertight bulkhead between its world and the world of common affairs. The emotions generated by amusement run their course within this watertight compartment.[11]

Aesthetic pleasure, even for the young, might derive not so much from the exclusive indulgence in agreeable emotions but from the excitement of discovery or the reassurance of having their intuitions articulated and endorsed.

The entertainer sets out to give the youngsters what he imagines they want and can take. There are others who use a developmental model to give the youngsters what they think is good for them. The educator is concerned not merely to discover the wavelength of the audience but to encourage the audience's personal growth. In so far as they are educational, the aims of the writers and theatre workers are similar to those of drama teachers in schools. Brian Way, as the educational theoretician of *Development Through Drama*, the theatrical theoretician of *Audience Participation* and as playwright, straddles both worlds and represents assumptions still current in Britain and widespread in America. Education is concerned with 'the individuality of individuals' and should concentrate on differences between people rather than upon samenesses. The direction of the individual's development depends upon some inner dynamic which the teacher can help to release. When this occurs, the subsequent activity is self-justifying. 'Drama' promotes all-round development but is of particular value in exercising the emotions. It ought to be said that Way has a preference for 'noble' emotions, though. Like 'drama', theatre for young people should be primarily concerned to 'stretch the heart'. It is for this that he devises his theory of audience participation. There are certain moments in a performance when the audience's collaboration is deliberately sought. As in the classroom, Way's precepts can encourage the use of 'exercise' as an end in itself, so in the theatre 'the action or activity is considered of central importance, while the reason or purpose for the action is of secondary value, being merely the excuse for the participation' (review by Chris Lawrence in *Drama Broadsheet*). The teacher and the theatre worker are engineering opportunities for 'self-expression'. In practice, though, the actual freedom an audience enjoys may be limited. The kind of participation being sought may be no more spontaneous than that of a pantomime audience and the presence of adults (making it a 'family audience') in both may call into question how far the child's response is his own and how far it is learned. Performing actions with the actor may do little to guarantee imaginative involvement with the play as a whole, and the audience may have only the illusion of being able to influence the direction of what is, after all, conceived as a complete theatrical artefact with a conclusion that is foregone.

In many respects, Way's idea of theatre for the young may not differ violently in practice from that of David Wood. Way's view of education, though, and of how theatre should further its ends, is not that of every or even most workers in the field. There are some who believe that the thinking side of the personality has its claims as a means to enlightenment and that too exclusive a concentration on the 'heart' can lead to sentimental self-indulgence. Gavin Bolton, a specialist in educational drama, also discerns a congruence of aim between drama teachers of a particular persuasion and certain theatrical companies: 'I make the point that whereas a drama teacher may have a range of objectives including social health, trust, skills etc., DIE and TIE share the same *principal* objective, that of bringing about a change in understanding.'[12] While the Way approach finds the theatrical theory and practice of the Stanislavsky of *An Actor Prepares* naturally congenial, Bolton's 'change in understanding' is the equivalent of the 'alienation' theory of Brecht, which recommends a kind of theatre that is 'open' and which encourages the audience not to become so absorbed in a performance that it cannot conceive alternative courses of action. Bolton is at pains to draw distinctions, too:

> An important difference between the two, however, is that whereas the learning area in drama may centre on the *theme* of the subject-matter, the *context* becoming but a pretext for opening up the theme, a TIE team must bring a different emphasis to the subject-matter. Their very skills as actors allow them to offer a rich context not normally available to the drama teacher, so that this work must be both contextually and thematically significant.[13]

Playwrights, either individually or in teams, may quite legitimately choose to begin with a 'theme'. I have heard the director of a TIE company describe her procedure as 'finding an issue and then looking for a context for it'. Shaw says that there is only one way of dramatising an idea and that is to put it into the mouth of someone who is obsessed with it. Starting with an issue may have the effect of simplifying the many-sidedness of experience but every dramatist simplifies to a greater or lesser degree. As Eric Bentley, talking of drama in general, puts it: 'It never lays claim to an interest in all of a man but only that part of him that is manifest in a chosen and partially fabricated Action.'[14]

It is when the desire to provide the young with food for thought overrides the concern for artistic truth that the 'context' fails to convince. But a committed (biased?) viewpoint can at least challenge a response. Some TIE companies are committed to political reform and their performances have the sort of content that would gladden Michael Billington's heart. They would claim, with some justification, that it is possible to involve even nine year olds in political issues if a truth about the power-structure of society can be encapsulated in an action or metaphor comprehensible to people with their knowledge and experience.

The danger comes when the eyes of the artist are closed to less palatable facts that the artistic process might throw up. It is then that what Brian Way calls 'mind-bending' occurs, and that is both bad education and bad art. As Collingwood says: 'If he begins by knowing what they are and uses his art for the purpose of converting others to them, he will not be feeding his Art on his political emotions, he will be stifling it beneath them.'[15]

Some playwrights, nervous of the charge or even the perpetration of 'bias', aim at objectivity. The result may be something like a Shavian debate without the redeeming wit. Roy Kift pours scorn on the 'worthy, balanced Theatre in Education' he sees around him.[16] Some playwrights consciously avoid politics altogether and in so doing lay themselves open to the charge of implicit 'conservatism'. David Wood, whose position is clearly stated in a letter: 'A balance must always be preserved, even if it means appearing to be a woolly middle-of-the-road sort', has been accused, in his play *The Plotters of*

Cabbage Patch Corner, of indulging in unconscious union-bashing, although he himself would stoutly maintain that the play will stand contradictory ways of playing. I am inclined to think that every play, whatever its intention, adopts an attitude to reality, but I am not sure that every attitude has political implications. John Arden, who is anything but politically neutral, sees 'balance' in aesthetic terms as a dramatic necessity:

> You try to see the other side, not out of a sort of wishy-washy liberalism, but simply because if you don't show the other side you aren't giving a true dramatic picture of the personal relationships, which is, after all, what the play is about. If you are dramatising a conflict and you say one side in my opinion is white, the other side is black, and you under-rate the strength, integrity and commonsense of the black side, then you will give your side an easy walkover. Well, you wouldn't be writing the play if your side had an easy walkover. It wouldn't be necessary to make this propaganda if there wasn't a serious struggle involved – therefore why not be fair?[17]

Paradoxically, exposing an audience to artistic truth may further the end of raising political consciousness more effectively than exposure to political assertion. Collingwood, again: 'There is only one condition on which a man can do good service to politics and to art. It is, that work of exploring and expressing one's political emotions should be regarded as serviceable to politics.'[18] This is as relevant to theatre for the young as to adult theatre. The would-be manipulator may get his fingers just as thoroughly burnt. Armed with parental prejudices, children are notoriously immune to easy conversion by other agencies. The best thing the educator can do is to make his plays as good as possible.

> Any good theatre will, of itself, be educational – i.e. when it initiates or extends a questioning process in its audience and, when it makes us look again, freshly, at the world, its institutions and conventions and at our place in that world, when it expands our notions of who we are, of the feelings and thoughts of which we are capable and our connection with the lives of others.[19]

To sum up. Plays for young people form a distinctive cultural category and are worthy of serious attention. What distinguishes them is the fact that, in content and in style, they consciously address themselves to an immature and less sophisticated audience, or at least an audience of a young age range. They represent a genuine art form in so far as they provide an experience which enlarges the audience's sympathies and awareness of human nature and human relationships. They stimulate the emotions, the mind and the imagination and afford both pleasure and 'education'. Such plays fall short in artistic integrity when playwrights and stage artists give undue attention to the effect they are trying to produce on an audience, whether to titillate them or bend their minds. There is a temptation, common among playwrights in general but particularly virulent among children's playwrights, to be more concerned with what the spectators are learning than with the truth of what is being expressed. Even with plays for the young, autonomy is an important artistic ideal – autonomy for the writer, for the performers and for the audience. The writer must be allowed his personal voyage of discovery, his personal fulfilment. As Joan Aiken says: '"What age group do you write for?" is a question frequently asked of children's writers and most of them tend to reply, "My own age".'[20] What satisfies the adult playwright as well as his young audience may end up appealing to the adults in audience, too.

What the writer should avoid, though, is the temptation to use his attempt to get inside the child's mentality to escape from being an adult. Coveney, writing of nineteenth-century literature, said: 'The child is now a symbol of growth and development and now a symbol of retreat into personal regression and self-pity.'[21] The opportunity and the danger apply to all writers for children.

2
History and Evolution

We have discussed the aesthetic standards that might legitimately be applied to theatre for the young and the factors, in general, that might influence its shape. In trying to account for its various manifestations at present in evidence, it is necessary to take a backward glance at its evolution. We shall have to look at social and political developments and at the status accorded to children at different times. Changes in educational theory and practice have had a profound effect on the range of dramatic experiences which have been offered. Developments in the theatre itself have provided a backdrop and, to some extent, supplied examples of possible content, form, organisation and philosophy. Funding, a crucial consideration in talking about any of the arts, is of peculiar significance in talking about a vulnerable phenomenon like theatre for young people. The esteem in which it is held is partially reflected in the willingness shown by sponsors, public or private, to bestow their patronage. Related to this is the attractiveness of working in this area to stage artists and playwrights of merit. These attractions have increased for the writer since publishers have extended their lists to include more and more plays for young audiences. Young people's theatre has improved its status and influence by organising itself into bodies such as SCYPT (Standing Conference of Young People's Theatre), BCTA (British Children's Theatre Association) and ASSITEJ (Association Internationale du Théâtre pour l'Enfance et la Jeunesse).

There may, as Aidan Chambers maintains, have been plays specially written for children throughout the centuries which have disappeared from existence, and we do know there have been pantomimes.[1] But for our purposes, it is in the present century that theatre for young people has come into its own. In 1904 there was *Peter Pan*, a play about childhood and children appealing both to the truly young and those wishing they were, drawing on pantomime conventions, including audience participation, and lending its weight to the association of youth with magic and fairies. However, before and during World War One, not a great deal in the way of new theatrical experience especially for young audiences was produced. But in 1914, Jean Stirling Mackinley did substitute plays for pantomimes, in itself an important departure. It was not until 1927 that the first regular professional company, the Scottish Children's Theatre, was founded by Bertha Waddell and subsequently permitted to perform in schools. In England, children had been paying their way into the Old Vic on Sundays since 1915 and the enterprise became grant-aided in 1924. On the political front, the establishment of County Borough Councils and Local Education Authorities in 1902 was to be highly significant for the future of funding, while in theatre at large, the agit-prop experiments of Piscator in Germany were spreading their influence to British companies. In 1929, the text of *Toad of Toad Hall* was published, a memorable adaptation, the first of many, of Kenneth Grahame's children's classic *Wind in the Willows*. It had many ingredients thought certain to appeal to young audiences, such as anthropomorphic animals, music and song and an implicit endorsement of the social status quo.

The 1930s witnessed the early work of Peter Slade, who first mooted a theoretical basis for participation work. He founded two companies, one in East Anglia in 1930–1 and one in London and the Home Counties in 1935. He was trying at this stage to reconcile spontaneous with artistically wrought drama. Later, he was to turn away from theatre, preferring what he called 'personal play' to 'projected play'. In 1937, Glasgow was the first Education Authority to make a grant to a company to produce performances in school of anything other than Shakespeare. The company was Bertha Waddell's. There were events of relevance in the adult theatre abroad. In the USA, the 1930s saw the emergence of the Living Newspaper, which inspired later developments in documentary theatre. In 1929, Brecht wrote and produced his Lehr Stücke, his 'teaching plays', exemplifying an 'open' form of drama which encouraged the audience to think of the world as dynamic rather than static, and changeable rather than God-ordained. The new play should make the audience think as well as feel.

It was the 1940s, though, before companies performing to children began to experiment. Some still saw entertainment and diversion as their *raison d'être*; others leaned more formally towards an educational role. Brian Way began to work for the Old Vic company and his seminal ideas on audience participation were crystallised. Another innovation of his for the time was his conscious attempt to match material with age-group or with the stage of development at which he judged the children to be. He also averred that the arena was the most propitious shape of acting area for audience involvement, moving away from the proscenium arch, with its curtained mysteries and imposing limits on the size of the audience with which it could cope. For Slade and Way, the school was the natural setting for children's performances. In 1944 an Education Act was passed which profoundly affected these institutions, introducing secondary education for all and attempting to encourage parity of esteem, a move in the direction of education geared to individual development. In the same year, Brian Way helped to form the West of England Children's Theatre Company, and the Compass Players, organised on a co-operative basis, toured the country bringing dramatic literature to life. But the Education Act had little immediate effect on the peripheral status of children's theatre as a cultural phenomenon.

In August 1946, the Arts Council of Great Britain was founded to continue in peacetime the work begun, with government support, in 1940, by the Council for the Encouragement of Music in the Arts (CEMA). Its stated objects were;

1. to develop and improve the knowledge, understanding and practice of the Arts;
2. to increase the accessibility of the Arts to the public throughout Great Britain;
3. to co-operate with government departments and other bodies to achieve these aims.

Some see the later function of the Arts Council as patron of children's theatre as the single most significant guarantee of that theatre's survival. The decade also contained the formation of John Allen's Glyndebourne Children's Theatre, John English's Midland Arts Centre in Birmingham, George Devine's Young Vic Players and Caryl Jenner's Mobile Theatre. Caryl Jenner's theatre began in 1948 under the wing of the Amersham Repertory Company and it toured schools until 1967, subsequently, as the Unicorn Theatre, becoming the first full-time professional theatre for children in London. Caryl Jenner campaigned for a purpose-built theatre on the South Bank. The following year, 1949, the Young Vic Players became a self-contained touring company, but it preferred to perform in theatre buildings. Like Caryl Jenner, Devine lamented the paucity of high-quality scripts.

Unfortunately, economy cuts in the early 1950s saw off some of these promising projects. Glyndebourne foundered, as did the Young Vic, and Caryl Jenner's company survived only by a gift. Most companies had to survive largely by box-office takings and, when possible, charitable trusts. There were compensations for the losses, however, and, with support from the Nuffield Foundation and the local authority, Brian Way's Theatre Centre opened in 1953. This enabled Way to continue his experiments with theatre form and with arena presentation and to use his own specially written material (such as *Pinocchio*). But if practical developments were few, theory flourished. In 1954, Peter Slade published *Child Drama*, a seminal book, which did much to wrench drama away from theatrical skills and towards child psychology. To Slade, children's drama did not need to express itself through adult conventions but could claim to be an art-form on its own. In this, it both fostered and resulted from growing trends towards child-centred education.

Spontaneity was valued at the expense of reflection and theatre for children received a theoretical demotion.

In the mid and late 1950s, theatre in general was subjected to an invigorating shake-up. *Waiting for Godot* in 1953 questioned the ability of even the adults to make sense of the world and and chose a form in which, as one critic put it, 'nothing happens – twice' to do it. The English Stage Company at the Royal Court established a writers' theatre and among these writers were Osborne, Wesker, Pinter and Arden. Osborne and Wesker, while showing a new sympathy with the attitudes and language of the working class or lower middle class, still preferred traditional naturalistic theatre. Pinter, acknowledging a debt to Noel Coward, added his own distinctive note of menace and portrayed the power struggle between individuals at a prepolitical stage, and Arden dealt with social and political themes in a form which owed much to Brecht. In the year of *Look Back in Anger* (1956), theatre for and by young people received a fillip when the National Youth Theatre was formed by Michael Croft. Although we are mainly concerned with theatre produced by adults for the young, the National Youth Theatre is interesting to us in so far as it attracted playwrights of the status of Peter Terson to write plays, for example *Zigger Zagger* and *Apprentices*, specifically addressed to its young audiences. In 1959, the British Children's Theatre Association was formed.

The 1960s was an era of expansion and innovation. The economy boomed and more money was available to workers in the field of young people's theatre. General awareness of the claims of young people increased and the pop world paid homage to young experience and to youthful spending power. Child-centred education gathered momentum and a congruence of the boom in drama in education and theatrical provision gave rise to Theatre in Education. Increasing numbers of writers of status turned their talents to improving available material, and publishers showed a greater willingness to publish the results in attractive form. Among the earliest of these writers were the Ardens with *The Business of Good Government* in 1960. In the same year the Ministry of Education recognised the National Youth Theatre as a national organisation and gave it grant aid. This was followed in 1963 by Local Education Authority support. Repertory theatres felt the need to present plays for children and made contact with schools. In 1965, ASSITEJ was launched. Now companies from the membership could interact with each other across national boundaries and confer at intervals with a view to sharing experience and improving both standards and standing.

For young people's theatre, perhaps the most signficant date was 1965. George Devine was at the Royal Court, and the Royal Court Studio was doing work with infants producing participation plays; but the most influential development occurred at Coventry. The management of the Coventry Civic Theatre, the Belgrade, and local teachers and the Local Education Authority got together to launch a pilot scheme, the aims of which are quoted by John O'Toole: 'We do not aim to create the social habit of theatre – it is an imaginative experience in its own right, an extension of the games children play in everyday life.'[2] Theatre is not something to learn about but something to learn *through*. Actors needed not only to be artists but to be teachers themselves. As important as the presentation was the preparation and the follow-up. The truly innovatory offering was the programme not the play. 'The terms "lesson" and "stage play" are replaced by the word "programme" as the experience will probably incorporate different and sometimes a greater variety of communication methods than will either the traditional lesson or the traditional play.'[3] This accorded with developments in education which stressed the unique value of the child's individual experience and insight rather than the social forms in which traditional theatrical statements had to be made. The swing in drama teaching was away from theatre as an end-product in favour of discovery through improvisation. The TIE programme deployed a form of participation that was far more open-ended and radical than Brian Way's (see p. 000). Even Way's 'directed' kind, which invited children in an audience to assist in the progress of the action, was, in effect, strictly limited in what it permitted. John O'Toole also identified three kinds of participation practised by TIE companies:

Extrinsic where the element of participation is separated from the theatricality.

Peripheral where the audience is invited to contribute in order to add to the theatricality without affecting either the structure and nature of the play or its own basic function as audience.

Integral where the audience perspective becomes also the perspective of the characters within the drama, especially when the audience members act as well as being acted upon. The structure of the dramatic conflict, the audience's relative position to it and therefore the total experience are altered. The element of theatre is no longer central.[4]

Extrinsic participation could include, say, post-performance discussion, and this can descend like a dead hand on the memory of the performance. Peripheral participation would still find a home in Way's scheme of things. But integral participation represents the unique contribution of TIE and it involves real power for the children to make of the experience what they will. O'Toole rhapsodises about all this and, as far as educational benefits are concerned, he has something to sing about:

> To appreciate the depths and power of belief which these techniques of total participation, well used, can engender, it is necessary only to see the sustained intensity which the children will put into those areas where they have freedom to respond how they will, and watch their unshakeable determination to resolve the hardest dilemma as well as their imaginative command of all the factors which may be relevant. There is no question that total experience is an enormously powerful one, by no means inferior to a 'purely' theatrical one, and its intensity remains with the children for a long time.[5]

Christine Redington goes further and asserts that, educationally speaking, the TIE programme is indubitably superior to the one-off theatrical performance:

> The questions that arise are: Why are we doing it? What use is it? In performing to hundreds of pupils and seeing them perhaps only once during their school careers, the work does not have any foundation to build on. To tour around, doing as many one-off performances as possible, is highly unsatisfactory, both for the schools and the company. The schools have no close liaison

> with the team, and little reason for building one. Many people would say that the one-off performances are better than nothing and that the theatrical event can, for a few pupils, be a satisfactory and lasting experience. Yet the companies' role in a school is unclear.
>
> This is one of the fundamental differences between theatre-orientated children's work and TIE. The latter is educationally motivated, closely linked with schools, the programmes are usually well followed up and fit into the school curriculum. Their preparation is often the result of some form of collaboration with teachers and the whole purpose for being in a school is clear. The itinerant role of the Young People's Theatre Company with no close relation with schools and no clear educational purpose can lead to muddled thinking in the preparation of programmes; actors unused to performing to children; unsuitable presentation; a reception as merely an entertainment, and a resulting lack of impact in a school.[6]

It is not appropriate here to argue which is educationally more efficacious, the complete play or the incomplete and malleable situation, although the teacher in me has some sympathy for the claims of O'Toole and Redington. In school or out, a play cannot be judged solely by what we 'learn' from it or through it. TIE companies have not eschewed the complete play as the 'trigger' or 'key' experience and our concern is with the effects, beneficial or deleterious, of all this extraneous activity on the nature and quality of the play as a work of art and with the work of art as a manifestation of a cultural development.

1965 was also the year when the Arts Council took official cognisance of theatre for the young. It set up a committee 'to enquire into the provision' of it 'in the widest terms, to make recommendations for further development and in particular to advise on the participation of the Arts Council in such work'.[7] Although it made grants to only five of the twelve professional theatre companies it listed, and although it commented that standards of material and work were generally low, it recognised the importance of such theatre and its recommendation of the need to subsidise it was a significant decision. Another was to set up a separate Young People's Theatre Panel. The report, *The Provision of Theatre for Young People*, was published in 1967 and the first grant of £90,000 was made. A boost was given to activity in the area and there was a spurt in growth, so much so that the National Council for Young People's Theatre was formed to coordinate it. There were TIE teams attached to repertory companies and increased efforts on the part of the reps themselves to make contact with schools. Greenwich Youth Theatre and the Bowsprit Company became Greenwich Young People's Theatre Ltd. The Unicorn Theatre got a six-year lease and Richard Gill dreamed his dream which was eventually to give rise to the Polka Theatre. In 1967 the burgeoning world of educational drama greeted the publication of one of its sacred texts, Brian Way's *Developmental Through Drama*. It is paradoxical that Way, one of the pioneers of modern children's theatre, should give birth to an anti-theatrical orthodoxy: drama in the classroom was engaged in for the benefit of those involved rather than for the benefit of the audience; being watched could encourage insincerity and exhibitionism. Dorothy Heathcote and Gavin Bolton, who took the movement in a somewhat different direction, are more honest in their arrogation of theatrical terms and devices and rehabilitate the 'showing', the reflection and discussion that Way downgraded. However, even they are less interested in the traditional play as a complete and closed artefact than in the 'situation' which, however clearly defined, is ultimately in the power of those attempting to learn through it. The teacher may open up adult perspectives but he is not a playwright in the established sense. Thus from the point of view of theatre as an art-form, the educational developments of the 1960s had a positive and a negative influence. Positively, they asserted the power of drama to enlighten and civilise the young and this had a spin-off for the status of children's theatre. Negatively, where 'theatre' is recognised as being important, it is a particular kind of construct or even a particular kind of play that is given preferential treatment. Nevertheless the scripted play showed its resilience, and between 1965 and 1972 big names were applying their talents to the writing of plays for young people to read and perform: Ted Hughes, Adrian Mitchell, Peter Terson, Joan Aiken and Ann Jellico. At a time when the serious theme or issue was the height of fashion, David Wood combined his talents with those of Sheila Ruskin to produce *The Owl and the Pussycat Went to See*, which relied on commercial appeal for its viability. Robert Bolt's play, *The Thwarting of Baron Bolligrew*, a fantasy story of the mission of Sir Oblong Fitzoblong to eradicate tyrannical Baron Bolligrew, enjoyed commercial success in the West End. Printing of works for young people began under the auspices of educational publishers: Bolt's play was published by Heinemann in 1966.

In the realm of international politics, 1968 saw a number of upheavals, from the May revolt of students and workers in France, police riots at the Democratic Convention in Chicago and race-riots and student sit-ins in other parts of the USA to the Spring uprising in Prague. In

1968, the Lord Chamberlain's power to censor theatrical performances was abolished and the gates opened (theoretically) to the admission of any subject for treatment. The 'fringe' movement had been gathering momentum, and between 1968 and 1973 experimental and political theatre groups increased in number. A reaction against mainstream theatre, which it saw as being a bourgeois institution enshrining middle-class values, fringe theatre took a wide variety of forms. It had certain characteristics in common, however. These were mainly the questioning of accepted priorities, an anti-illusory approach to theatrical presentation and a concern to challenge the dominance of the word over the action and the image. Former rebels like Osborne and Wesker came to look part of the establishment they had knocked and even the Royal Court was seen as a 'writer's theatre'. Not only was the dominance of the playwright challenged but also the dominance of the director. Some companies formed themselves into co-operatives where directing and writing were jobs that could rotate. Writing might be restricted to a scenario and a play might evolve through group improvisation. Actors' companies were formed. The London Arts Laboratory and Charles Marowitz's Open Space were launched. Ed Berman founded Inter Action Trust, which was a centre to encourage and assist community action and which used theatrical techniques to create collaborative performances with a child audience. It is possible, however, that Berman's work is significant more for its sociological than its artistic impact.

The combined funding of the Arts Council and the Local Authorities meant that new specialist young people's companies could be formed in places such as Bolton, Leeds, Edinburgh and Greenwich. There was a Youth Theatre Policy statement. The late 1960s and early

1970s saw the involvement of the big companies also. The Royal Shakespeare Company formed Theatreground. In the spirit of optimism abounding in the late 1960s, and under the umbrella of the National Theatre, the Young Vic was revived in 1970.

With the boom in the economy went a boom in theatre building. New repertory theatres opened in Leeds (1970) and Sheffield (1971), widening the scope of work for the young as well, whether this was done in schools or in the theatres themselves. In the sphere of alternative theatre, new venues, such as the Royal Court Theatre Upstairs, the ICA and the Open Space, were opened and new repertory theatres incorporated studios to house new experiments. For Young People's Theatre work specifically, there was the Cockpit Studio Theatre, home of the Cockpit Arts Workshop and financed by the Inner London Education Authority. It was the first public theatre in London to be designed for drama, music and mixed media performances for 300 years.[8] It also became a model for the many new studio theatres where, eventually, theatre for the young could be given a showcase performance. In 1970, the Young Vic got its own building. The National Youth Theatre found a base in the Shaw Theatre. Caryl Jenner died in 1973, and her successor, Matyelok Gibbs, struggled hard to win a permanent base for the Unicorn Theatre in Southwark.

A new phase of TIE development began with the formation of a separate team organisation at Leeds and its subsequent detachment, physically and artistically, from the main house, and of teams at Nottingham and Peterborough. At the Arts Council, the Young People's Theatre Panel was amalgamated with the Drama Panel (both testifying to its responsibility and threatening its independence).

At this time, some repertory companies used the extra money allocated for young people's work to mount Shakespearean productions. Much of the touring work was based on (often established) scripts. There were new plays but the range of quality and seriousness was wide. Pam Brighton was producing Ann Jellico's work at the Royal Court. In 1972, the year before Roundabout was formed under Sue Birtwhistle, I wrote a somewhat stilted and earnest play for the Nottingham Playhouse Company called *Maoris, Missionaries and Muskets*, about the impact of evangelism and firearms on Polynesian culture and society. It toured the county's secondary schools and achieved one performance in the main house and a review in *The Times Educational Supplement*. At the time, such a venture could be a step on the ladder for professional actors of the stature of Ron Cook, providing they did not linger on it long enough to stultify. The show was seen by Joan Mills, who reigned at the Royal Court from 1972 to 1976 and founded the Young Writers' Festival, and she was impressed not by the history but by the Maori chants and dances, believing, as she told me in a letter, that young people's theatre had to rival their pop music in excitement. At Bolton, *Sweetie Pie*, a play about a serious modern issue, women in society, came into being by a different process, being devised by the company (and subsequently published in 1975). Much TIE work was still largely performance based, despite the accumulation of follow-up projects around the performances. In the same year (1972) Ken Campbell wrote a play called *Old King Cole* for Peter Cheesman at Stoke. Formally eschewing stage animals and 'Magic', Campbell created a 'potty *Beano* world' revolving round the 'pantomime robbers', Faz and twoo. Despite the temptations the writing of fantasy can involve, the tone of the play is remarkably unsentimental and unpatronising. This play, too, was eventually rewarded with the permanence of print.

By 1973, well over half the regional rep theatres were doing some kind of work in schools and, writing in 1974, Moses Goldberg, from his transatlantic perspective, could observe that children's theatre in Britain was 'booming'. The Young Vic was at the peak of its international reputation, and the Arts Council and the National Theatre agreed that it should become an independent body.

A group of Her Majesty's Inspectors launched a survey of the work of theatre companies in schools (resulting in the publication in 1977 of DES Survey 22: *Actors in Schools*). It emerged that many YPT companies had begun to incorporate theatre for the community at large in their output. In 1967, it had been decreed that a proportion of the Arts Council grants to repertory theatres should be ear-marked for work for young people, but with the ending of this procedure in 1974 the reps as a whole allocated progressively less. To protect their interests *vis-à-vis* the funding bodies, several TIE and YPT companies formed themselves into the Standing Conference of Young People's Theatre. SCYPT was also to represent them at major national and international conferences and 'to promote debate, the sharing of ideas and experiences and to further the general aims of the movement'.[9] The kind of play favoured among the membership was that which challenged the established order of society and sometimes issued in left-wing polemic. Power in one of the bastions of traditional ideas changed hands as David Johnston took over from Brian Way as Director of the Theatre Centre in 1976, resulting also in a change of programme and philosophy. The new regime was to give preference to plays about 'social situations young people encounter today'.

At about this time, various companies came into being as a result of the Job Creation Scheme, but they were very vulnerable to government cuts. Such a one was the Daylight Theatre Company of Gloucestershire, which started at the instigation of the local drama adviser and after a year became – in self-defence – an independent business. The Company's speciality was highly didactic plays recommending energy conservation. They came in for commissions from the Department of Energy, eventually, and got a free van from Shell, putting on as many as 160 performances a term, and touring extensively.

Working with the M6 Theatre Company of Rochdale, David Holman wrote *No Pasaran*, a play about Fascism in Britain, and it was performed at the Bolton Studio Theatre. If theatre for the young were to name its 'quality' writers, Holman's name would be high on the list. He is a man who has made a speciality of writing carefully crafted pieces which encapsulate an important issue in a detailed and particular situation, finding the focus that provides a young audience with the way in. *No Pasaran* concentrates on the figure of a Jewish boxer in Germany and England and allows anti-Semitism to manifest itself in relation to him. In 1975, Coventry TIE Company produced a complete play about the case of Craig and Bentley called *Example* (which was published in 1980).

But if the play dealing with contemporary issues was popular in educational circles, another kind of children's play was proving resilient and another 'specialist' playwright establishing himself. 1976 saw the first production of David Wood's *The Gingerbread Man*, a fantasy entertainment which has become a hardy perennial. In 1977, myth and legend from Ancient Greece were given an impressive airing by John Wiles, who, in response to a commission from the Cockpit Arts Workshop for its eighth annual youth production, wrote *The Golden Masque of Agamemnon* to be performed in the round. Counter to contemporary trends, *The Golden Masque* unashamedly endorsed the notion of heroism. Michael Bogdanov was packing them in the Cottesloe and Lyttleton auditoriums of the National Theatre with his productions of *Under Milk Wood*, *Gawaine and the Green Knight* and *Antigone*. (In the following year, Bogdanov was to take over from Denise Coffey at the Young Vic.) At this time, the National Theatre together with the Royal Shakespeare Company were receiving 40 per cent of the Arts Council Grant.

In 1977, the Drama Panel of the Arts Council formed a Children's Theatre Working Party. 'Its report recorded an increasing volume and variety of work, especially in Theatre in Education. It strongly recommended increased funding and new collaborative structures with the Regional Arts Associations and with local Authorities. But the report was neither published nor systematically implemented.'[10] In the following year, though, David Wood and John Gould launched *Flibberty and the Penguin*. Hitherto having to rely heavily on box-office receipts, Wood finally earned an Arts Council grant and achieved a breakthrough in his ambition to run a national children's touring company, performing not in schools but in theatres.

It was also in 1977 that Nick Barter was appointed (for what was to be an influential ten years) as Director of the Unicorn Theatre in London. Two years later, Richard Gill's 'dream' became reality with the official opening, also in London, of his palace of dreams, the Polka Children's Theatre, with him in charge. But 1979 was to prove a pivotal year in other respects too.

3
The Present Scene

The 1960s and 1970s had witnessed a great liberalisation in attitudes towards and treatment of theatre, both for the 'mature' and the young. The present scene can conveniently be dated from 1979, the year the Conservative Government under Margaret Thatcher was elected. The new right-wing radicalism, which ushered in the entrepreneurial society, had an impact on the nature of some and the viability of virtually all theatrical endeavours. Public expenditure was cut, there was rate-capping and accountability, the Arts Council was starved of adequate funds and the Metropolitan Borough Councils, which had been sympathetic towards the underprivileged and generous towards minority groups, were eventually abolished. In a climate where profitability is the touchstone, theatre for young people is particularly at risk. Main-stream theatre, looking to its own survival, may be tempted to do the minimum for young audiences. Well-established TIE and YPT companies also found their existence threatened, companies such as M6, Harrogate and Wolsey and even the famous, epoch-making Coventry Belgrade TIE Company. Commercial sponsorship started to grow, with its attendant dangers to independence and its relative unreliability. Some felt society was shifting towards a transatlantic model.

Every year in New York, there is a showcase of excerpts from the work of various children's theatre companies from all over the USA. Representatives of interested firms, libraries, museums and so on come to watch and the performers try to win their financial support. I went to New York in 1983 to see one for myself. Most of the material was predictable and safe – fairy-stories, more adaptations of *Wind in the Willows* and *Tom Sawyer* with mandatory music, song and (with the aid of a Broadway choreographer) dancing. The Performing Arts Repertory Theatre of New York did its educational stint with another biographical play, this time of Einstein's life. The token challenge was represented by *Freedom Train*, Marvin Gordon's dramatisation of the legend of Harriet Tubman, who was instrumental in executing the release of Negro slaves by means of the so-called 'underground railroad'. One could argue that even this was safe as it showed a charismatic figure performing her miracles rather than – as some authorities think is the case – the slaves themselves, using their initiative and courage. Altogether, there was, in the showcase, more evidence of Disney than of Brecht. Even in the USA, though, there is some state subsidy as in the New York State Council for the Arts, and the individual who wishes to sponsor an arts organisation or event can take advantage of the fact that up to 10 per cent of pre-tax profit is exempt from tax.

In Britain, the Arts Council, willy-nilly, is going to represent the lifeline for most theatrical companies. It has to play the part of intermediary between the petitioning artists and the paymaster government. When Sir William Rees-Mogg was appointed chairman in 1982, there were widespread misgivings about whether he would incline towards Government philosophy, but he declared his intention of following in the footsteps of Keynes, a famous predecessor, and lobbying for more state aid. An interpretation of subsequent events may have justified scepticism as to his willingness or ability to carry out his promise. The first part of the decade saw the Arts Council building up to the publication of its policy document: *The Glory of the Garden* in 1984. Later in the same year, in tandem with the Council of Regional Arts Association Drama Officers, it organised a national conference on 'Theatre and Education' at the University of Warwick to which a galaxy of delegates from a wide range of backgrounds was invited. The aim was to canvass opinion as to the policy proposals on theatre for the young and Theatre in Education. To lay the foundations of informed discussion, eight regional conferences were arranged prior to Warwick.

The main thrust of *The Glory of the Garden* is towards devolution, decentralisation. The idea had been around for a long time but for the Arts Council it represented a reconsideration of its function. More responsibility was to be passed over to the Regional Associations and the local authorities. Since government funds were still tight, spreading the money around meant robbing Peter (old 'revenue clients') to pay Paul. But Peter's pence were not to be sloshed around the regions for the benefit of just any company that set itself up to purvey entertainment and enlightenment: it was to be targeted on 'centres of excellence'. The Crucible Theatre in Sheffield was the main beneficiary and its new assistant-director, with major influence over the development of work for young people, and a man formidably well qualified in educational theatre, Mike Kay, expressed his wish that the TIE company, Vanguard, should become a 'permanent' company which, as well as commissioning new works with special reference to local needs, would, as the Arts Council hoped, give an airing to the best work of other companies. He made an early start with a showcase consisting of *Raj* (evolved at Leeds), *No Pasaran* (M6, Rochdale) and *Pow Wow* (Belgrade, Coventry). The companies to make the sacrifices which would allow the redistribution of largess were not merely the big national theatre and opera companies but TIE/YPT companies such as M6 and well-known adult 'fringe' companies such as 7:84. On the other hand, the Arts Council recognised the need for a special fund for children's and young people's theatre and increased funding for black and Asian drama. Another new initiative was the introduction of 'challenge' funding by which the Arts Council would match any acquisition of support that the company was enterprising enough to solicit from local communities. Many questions are begged, of course, by the language of a document like *The Glory of the Garden*, not least of which is the critieria which the council applies in determining who deserves support and who does not. What is 'excellence'? Are companies being tested for their ability to balance the books? Is their political soundness in question, and, if so, from what political standpoint? What artistic criteria, if any, are invoked? Sir William Rees-Mogg, in his introduction to *The Glory of the Garden*, attempts to define the way the Arts work and account for the demand for them.

> One does not have to paint the modern world black to see one reason for that demand. Modern societies, even in democracies and much more so in totalitarian states – is depersonalised by the scale of its organisa-

> tion, a scale which is being exploded by information technology. The Arts, human, creative, inspiring, individual, warm, alive, provide a natural healing to this sense of depersonalisation and the appreciation of beauty can transcend the moon-like chill of our electronic world. For those of religious faith the human creativity of the Arts can be a way of sensing the beauty of God's creation.

One wonders what kind of children's play would satisfy these romantic demands for warmth, reassurance and beauty. Those writers and performers who believe the Arts should disturb and challenge (even) children might be forgiven for looking ruefully at the state of their pockets.

The national conference in Warwick in the summer thrashed out a significantly concerted response to *The Glory of the Garden*, and, at its plenary session, drew up its own proposals and resolutions. It thought the aim of those with influence should be 'the establishment of national provision for TIE/YPT as a free service throughout Great Britain'. It demanded immediate reversal of the Arts Council decision to withdraw funding from M6 and the Harrogate company. Showcases should become a regular phenomenon. 'Criteria for assessment should be re-examined jointly by practitioners, educators and funding bodies and procedures should be open.' The Arts Council should 're-introduce ear-marking of specific funds for TIE/YPT. After attention had been drawn to their plight in the United Nations Year of the Disabled Person (1981) the integration of disabled people with the rest of the community should be furthered by the Arts Council in undertaking to support Graeae and other companies working in the field.' To make reforms possible, the Arts

Council was required to make a vigorous approach to Government for more money.

In response to the recommendations of the conference, the Arts Council, jointly with the Regional Arts Associations, issued a new policy statement in 1986, bringing the public up to date with what interim initiatives it had taken.

> Subsequent implementation of the first stages of this strategy has enabled some development of existing companies and an initial establishment of at least two new Theatre in Education companies. These developments were funded from the increased allocation to the Arts Council's Drama budget and, in some cases, from increased funds to the Regional Arts Associations . . . . These funds have been materially increased by 'challenge funding' responses from local authorities. It is hoped that there will be further commitment to this area of work in future stages of the strategy.[1]

Although it was not mentioned, M6 and Harrogate were reprieved. Most of the proposals made at the Warwick Conference were endorsed and action was promised. Generally, the document was a statement of intent, though, of what the Council would strive to achieve in partnership with the Regional Arts Associations, plugging gaps in national provision. Also, it would stimulate new writing for young people's work and support training for theatre practitioners and teachers to get the most out of YPT. On the subject of quality, it says: 'The specific criteria for assessing Theatre for Young People will take into account the criteria of the appropriate funding bodies, the aims and objectives of the companies and, above all, the needs of the audiences.'

Writing in the *Guardian* in 1985, Tom Sutcliffe sees the real but undeclared criteria as being commercial. If the recipients of support make a profit, bully for them. If not, let them not come whinging. Challenge funding was mere 'window dressing', and the true purpose of *The Glory of the Garden* was to merit Mrs Thatcher's endorsement. Rees-Mogg has toed the Government line and his secretary-general, Luke Rittner, had a 'management consultant's brief – to see the Arts Council as a business and make it more business-like'. Keeping to the budget was all that mattered, really. Sutcliffe saw Rittner as lacking 'passionate engagement with the Arts and proper appreciation of what they are for. This is part of the pattern with the low calibre of councillors and specialist panels.'

The net result of this for the artistic life of the nation was to encourage artists not to take risks and to discourage 'artistic daring'. In the second article in this *Guardian* series on the state of the Arts, Nicholas de Jongh describes how Lord Gowrie, Minister for the Arts, had pinned his hopes on business but the Inland Revenue was killing incentives to potential donors. (This is where the USA scores.) Rate-capping would limit what local authorities could do. In the third article, Anthony Field, who had been Finance Director of the Arts Council for twenty-seven years, tried to spike the Government's guns by arguing that investment in the Arts brings rich financial rewards.

The supply of money is obviously vital to the continued existence of a theatrical company and it is obviously and fundamentally relevant to any survey (such as this) of an aspect of cultural life over a period of time. But the level of funding does not automatically correlate with the quality of artistic product. We have observed that a degree of autonomy is indispensable if the artist is to record the truth as he sees it. And what are the 'needs' of a young audience and how can we be confident we can gauge them? Might we not end up pitching our play too low and patronising them? Do involvement of educationalists, educational training on the part of the artists and theatrical exposure on the part of teachers guarantee that there will be an artistic product and not merely a framework for the exploration of 'issues'? One cannot ultimately account for the emergence of or frustration of high-quality art solely in terms of social, political, financial or educational context. But although one cannot completely account for quality, one can observe the effect of the setting on content and form.

While theatre companies were being encouraged to liberate themselves from their dependence on official subsidy, a new authoritarianism was making its presence felt and with it a deployment of power to decree what the public, 'mature' or young, should be allowed to see. One of the adult companies, 7:84, which was sentenced to be eradicated from the glorious garden, put on Miles Malleson's play *Six Men of Dorset* at the time of the miners' strike. Collecting boxes for the miners' cause (at the Crucible Theatre, Sheffield, where I saw it) were thrust under the noses of the departing audiences. John McGrath, founder of the company, was convinced that there was official animus against them and that that animus was political and from the right. In October 1984, he said so in the *Guardian*: 'the confusion, self-congratulation and mendacity of their fictional "reasons" for cutting 7:84 have convinced anybody who has studied them that the real reason is political distaste'. He goes on:

> It is a matter for some alarm when the guardians of our culture appear to have made it impossible for a work of

> art with a particular message to be made at all. Especially when those guardians have astonishingly little qualification for making artistic judgments of any kind apart from their adherence to a political elite, an elite itself incapable of inspiring any work of art with or without a purpose.

Anthony Field, at whom McGrath had a personal snipe, denied any political motive and ascribed it to the sheer profusion of fringe companies that subsidies should, in all fairness, be rotated, and he firmly asserted that 'intrinsic merit' was the main criterion that the Arts Council applied to the works of its supplicants. It is difficult to sort out who is right. All I can say is that the production of Malleson's play seemed to me to have considerable artistic integrity which was not compromised by its obvious relevance to current events in the mining world.

A couple of years or so later, Jim Allen's play *Perdition*, which contained an attack on Zionist involvement with the Nazi Jew-baiters, was taken off before it was put on, so to speak. The theatre responsible for encouraging the axing was none other than the Royal Court itself, which had formerly fought so valiantly against the depredations of the Lord Chamberlain. As with 7:84, the same claim was made that the play was aborted on aesthetic grounds, but there were hints and accusations to the effect that pressure was brought to bear by influential Zionists with power to damage the Royal Court's interests abroad. This time nobody was allowed to see the play, and make, however humble, a personal and independent judgement.

Another paymaster, the Local Authority, which John McGrath avers has 'even more political volatility than the Arts Council' was making its contribution. In 1982, the Doncaster Arts Co-operative (founded three years previously with Manpower Services Commission money) proposed to tour Trevor Griffiths's play, *Oi for England*, around venues in South Yorkshire. The play is about a skinhead band which is invited to play at a concert which will clearly front a racialist rally. There are powerful passages of anti-black rhetoric, but, in the end, one member of the group joins the Asian daughter of their landlord to resist racialism on the streets. This time, though, the censors were Labour Councillors and the audiences deemed to be in need of protection those of young people. Councillor Brown, chairman of South Yorkshire's Recreation Committee, was worried that the young might be influenced in favour of the National Front rather than by the built-in condemnation that the play contains. The Chairman declared that the councillors were intelligent enough to make their own artistic judgement and that he would insist that they had prior access to scripts if the supplicant was an itinerant company. Like John McGrath, Ron Rose, Director of the DAC saw that the preferential treatment given to building-based at the expense of touring groups would effectively draw the sting of adventurous theatre. Certainly the assumption of infallibility of artistic judgement (the implicit basis for censorship) is a worrying thing, even when exercised nominally for the protection of children.

Plays intended for performance to young people also suffered from the blue pencil and scissors of the censor. Perversely enough, however one might dislike this treatment, at least it shows that such plays were likely to make an impact and were worthy of attention. Would-be censors of art for the young have reason to feel more confident of the justice of their actions (in their eyes, at least). One might fairly say, with the censorship of adult art, that it fails to acknowledge that would-be recipients are responsible adult people. But how can you expect adult responsibility in people who are manifestly not adult yet? One might retort that if you do not treat them as if they were sensible and grown-up, they never will be. Perhaps writers, directors, actors, teachers and parents ought to take especial care with children to ensure that what they see and hear is something they can comprehend. But to argue that because a play is about a contentious or sensitive subject, it should on those grounds be withheld from presentation discounts the integrity of the artists. Because a play expresses strongly held convictions does not necessarily mean that a young audience will be incapacitated from thinking and feeling for themselves. I went to see *Example*, the TIE play about the trial and execution of Derek Bentley in 1952, performed in a school in Nottinghamshire by the Roundabout team. When we were leaving the auditorium at the end, I overheard two lads of about fourteen commenting on the show. One said: 'I thought we were going to be the jury.' The other said: 'I'd have hanged him', a view in direct opposition to the thrust of the play. A play that is informed with a sense of outrage might still recognise that a case has to be made and might feel that its best chance of drawing attention to its views is to convince the imagination of the audience that its 'evidence' is valid. Any play needs to *earn* its right to be heard, and the artists who create it need to allow their own prejudices to be constantly tested against what can be made to work in a theatre. But those judging it ought to be humble enough to give it a chance and to look carefully at their own motives for accepting or rejecting it.

In September 1983, a conference was held in Oxford on peace and conflict studies. It emerged that a large amount of peace studies was being taught in schools and that it was not by any means being done universally under the official title. Conservative and Labour councils felt that peace studies was not a legitimate subject and some delegates were worried that such a subject might prove a thin disguise for propaganda on behalf of the Campaign for Nuclear Disarmament.

In the same year, Theatre Centre launched its Festival of Peace. By coincidence the Greater London Council was holding its Peace Year and Theatre Centre came in for some timely sponsorship. Theatre Centre offered three plays by David Holman. *Peacemaker* was about two groups of people, the Reds and the Blues, divided by a wall. Each group expresses ignorant prejudice against the other until, one day, two little red girls see a blue person signalling to them from the other side. Eventually they all meet and make friends, but a guard comes and forces them to block up the hole they made in the wall – but it is not completely blocked. *Susumu's Story* is set in Hiroshima just before and when the atomic bomb is dropped. It shows the tragic effects of the action on ordinary Japanese families and ends with a plea to the audience:

> Today there are bombs in the world which are far more powerful than the one which fell on us. We of Hiroshima, the city that died, are pledged to make a world free of these weapons so that there are no more to die like us. But it cannot be done just by us.

The third Holman play, *1983*, was about the siting of cruise-missiles in Britain later that year. In characteristic Holman style, it avoids direct debate on the rights and wrongs and focuses on a concrete and recognisable situation. It is set near a US Air Force base in Suffolk where local girl, Steff, marries an American serviceman, Carl.

Her schoolteacher friend, somewhat self-righteous Viv, has come to demonstrate against the base and particularly the missiles and she alerts Steff to the consequences of nuclear war. Carl, who learns with mounting horror what his driver's job really entails, also has his complacency shattered and both of them are forced to take stock.

Norman Tebbit, the Employment Secretary in the Thatcher Government, discovering that these plays were taking place in his Essex constituency, condemned them as 'at best irrelevant and at worst decidedly harmful',[2] being propaganda, he averred, for unilateral nuclear disarmament. He had neither seen the plays nor asked to be allowed to read a script, but he advised parents to keep their children away from school to prevent their being corrupted. He certainly gave YPT a publicity boost and David Johnston, Director of Theatre Centre, was interviewed on television. With the exception of the *Daily Mail* and the *Sun* in particular, the papers were by and large critical of Mr Tebbit, taking him to task for urging parents to break the law by encouraging truancy. His advice was generally ignored.

Most interesting from our point of view is the stimulus the attempted censorship gave to papers to seek artistic grounds on which to defend – and attack – the plays. The *Daily Telegraph* (29 March 1983) quoted David Johnston as saying that they 'deliberately played down any horrific aspects and came to no definite conclusion'. The *Sunday Times* (30 May) praised *1983* for 'avoiding emotional extremes' and went on to say: 'The aim of *1983* as an educational tool is to open up a debate even if its view of the matter is clear and Roger Watkin's production does so with effective theatrical means. That is the art of this propaganda and I would say the GLC is getting its money's worth.' In other words it *does* reach a definite conclusion but in the Lawrentian sense of leading the sympathies towards what is alive and away from things gone dead. For a play to be a satisfying experience it needs to make an impact irrespective of educational follow-up or exploration of 'issues'. Rosalind Carne (*Guardian* 3 May), reviewing the performance at the Drill Hall, waxed very enthusiastic about its theatrical merits:

> Painted costumes by Sue Hill give the whole affair a storybook air, mildly dream-like and fantastical and emphasising, by contrast, the all-too-real subject matter. It is an unusual juxtaposition which, together with the moments of personal intimacy in an impersonal world, suggested it would make good television drama.
>
> We share in the rising consciousness of Carl (Calvin Simpson), a black airman, from Chicago, and his sensitive English wife, Steff. They are married in 1979, during the attempted raid on the US embassy in Tehran, and the ceremony is interrupted by an alert at the base. From that moment on, their carefree partnership is haunted by the spectre of destruction. Bombers roar overhead as Steff's friend Viv showers her with confetti in the absence of a husband, one of several striking theatrical moments.
>
> Best of all – or rather that which gives most food for nightmares – is Carl's training programme. Seated in the mock-up cabin of a 40-ton truck he stares into a video which reconstructs his imaginary drive into Europe's doomsday. Out of the bunker and down the road, round the S-bend and into the forest where he is to let loose his four 'babies' towards the USSR. Women and children block the road in protest. He stops. The trainer tells him to go through the exercise again, and this time he doesn't falter.

City Limits (2 June) found it 'a sombre play, but performed with great crispness and humour which brings the debate down to human terms'. A. J. Johnson, Chairman of the Governors at a primary school in Cheshire, wrote to the *Daily Telegraph* (12 April) to complain that *Susumu's Story* was promoting propaganda and felt that it 'was nebulous in its story line', particularly for the age group at which it was aimed. 'Finally I would stress that the sound effects were unnecessarily loud, especially in the scene where the bomb "exploded" and several children were disturbed and alarmed by this.' A parent, Paul Burn, though, writing to the *Guardian* (31 March), examined his daughter on the subject of what 'meanings' she had extracted from *Peacemaker*: the daughter said –

> There were once two groups of people: the Reds and the Blues. They had a silly quarrel and built a wall between. One day, one of the Reds threw a ball over the wall while she was learning to juggle. A Blue threw it back and they made friends on the spot. They started to pull the wall down, but a guard made them rebuild it. They did so, but taking care to leave one brick out. Through this gap they exchanged their hats. The End.

Mr Burn comments as follows:

> My six-year-old daughter says there were more bits but she can't remember them. This is the substance of one of the plays being shown to Waltham Forest schoolchildren that oddly offends Mr Tebbit (*Guardian*, March 29). As you can see it is ridden with CND propaganda, and we expect our daughter to board the bus to Greenham Common any day.

The atomic bomb is a fearful thing and the arousal of fear (*vide* Aristotle) can lead to enlightenment in an audience. Children are used to fearful monsters in their own fairy-tales, nursery rhymes and games and on television. One does not come to terms with fear by pretending it does not exist and *Susumu's Story* did not violate dramatic credibility by promising an easy victory.

Reviewing a production of *Peacemaker* in 1987 by Theatre About Glasgow, Joyce McMillan found the play 'an unremarkable piece of work'. If it is indeed artistically unremarkable, that would tend to weaken any propagandist effects. Plays are metaphors, anyway, and unless the metaphor enshrines some truth about experience, the play may be diverting but not dangerous.

In the sensitive atmosphere of the early 1980s, Cockpit's programme, *The Pitcher Plant*, of which the aim was to enable fourth- and fifth-year pupils 'to explore sex and sexual feelings' was banned after a pilot run, this time by an Assistant Education Officer of the Inner London Education Authority. In an open letter to him, the Cockpit team said: 'We view the censorship of our work as a political act made by those people who are responding to the needs of this Tory Government to curtail and smash the gains made in Education, in order to force through cuts in Health, Education and the Social Services.' In Ipswich, Wolsey TIE team proposed to put on a version of *A Midsummer Night's Dream* that would examine the problems of sexism. The play was to be called: *Antidote to Dream*. Although it did some touring, the team, in a plea for support from SCYPT, claimed that 'attempts are being made to undermine our bookings and the confidence of the teachers, not only in the programme but the professional ability of the team itself' by the Senior English Adviser and the Area Drama Adviser. The conflict ended with the sacking of the three permanent members of the company. Gazebo TIE Company, funded by the Manpower Services Commission, chose to reject most of their grant in 1984 because they were ordered to submit details of any proposed programme prior to producing it. In effect, this meant voluntary reduction of the size of the team.

In 1986, Perspectives Theatre Company, based in Mansfield, ran into trouble when they set about producing a play for young people of fifteen and over, in the East Midlands area, called *Best of Friends* by Noel Greig. In their newsletter they said: 'the play deals with such issues as the economic policies of the postwar government, unemployment, arms spending, cancer research, life in the forces, friendship and gay sexuality'. The Director of Education for Nottinghamshire County Council banned the play from all schools in the county. Since no other satisfactory reason was given, the company was forced to conclude that objection was being made to some of its content – most likely the gay sexuality. In the end, a group of County Councillors agreed to watch a performance and, as a result, the ban was lifted. In any case, the play was currently being toured around various community centres unmolested. The merits of the play in performance will be considered later but the company deserve some credit for their attempt to look boldly at a contentious subject. When the return to Victorian values is the war-cry in high places, anything which dares to say that homosexuality is not, *per se*, a sin is a welcome counterbalance.

But by 1987, when *Best of Friends* was performed by Sheffield Crucible Vanguard Company, the censors were all set to acquire a new set of teeth in the form of the proposed Local Authority Bill, Clause 28 of which stated:

1. A local authority shall not
   (a) promote homosexuality or publish material for the promotion of homosexuality
   (b) promote the teaching in any maintained school of the acceptability of homosexuality as a pretended family relationship by the publication of such material or otherwise
   (c) give financial assistance or other assistance to any person for either of the purposes referred to in (a) and (b) above.
2. Nothing in subsection 1 above shall be taken to prohibit the doing of anything for the purpose of treating or preventing the spread of disease.

The extent of the threat to artistic freedom depends, of course, on how you interpret the word 'promote'. It could imply that the mere inclusion of homosexual subject matter in a play, irrespective of the attitude the audience was invited to take, could be interpreted as encouraging, condoning and publicising undesirable behaviour. This could effectively put a stop to the activities of the likes of Mr Greig.

The Standing Conference of Young People's Theatre felt alarmed enough at the growing trend to devote its Annual Conference in September 1983 to the topic: 'Dealing with Censorship', addressing itself to questions such as 'Can we recognise censorship?' 'How does censorship work?' 'What forms does it take?' 'Can it ever be justified?' The Conference took the form of a simulation in which the delegates were divided into Actors, Censors and Teachers, and they were told a state of emergency had been declared. As a focus and a source of ideas for the actors devising their play, a performance of *ABC*, a play about Nicaragua by David Holman, was presented by

Theatre Centre. No glib answers were suggested but there was a body of opinion that the only effective action was political and that that might involve the workers taking power. *ABC* took a sympathetic view of the left-wing Sandinistas; but while Perspectives' *Best of Friends* was eating the bitter bread of banishment, Holman's play was touring schools without a stain on its character. Needless to say, SCYPT was very vocal, when the time came, in its opposition to the Local Authorities Bill.

If one tries to give a broad picture of the range of organisation producing theatre for the young at this juncture and of the kinds of artistic offerings they initiate or accommodate, one is inclined to agree with Christine Redington that one is faced with a 'rather diverse, somewhat confusing scene'.[3] Some groups, like their adult 'fringe' cousins, are organised as collectives, with no permanent director and with everybody having the chance to fulfil a variety of functions and be paid the same money (for example Perspectives). There are political implications in the very structure, and members of these companies will freely confess to being in the business for the sake of making their contributions to political change (in a leftward direction). Others, like York YPT, may have a manager but his oversight of group productions may be restricted to a last-minute polish. They may be a component of a provincial repertory theatre or they may (like Leeds TIE) operate independently. Merseyside YPT claimed to

> seek cooperation with teachers through a management structure unique in Britain. Legally we are a non-profit limited company and a charity. The company is owned and controlled by its members, the shareholders, who must be Merseyside teachers. Purchase of a £5.00 share

> entitles members to elect and serve on the Council of Management which determines policy, decides which plays are put on and takes final responsibility for the financial affairs of the company, but the final say is with teachers on behalf of young people at school.[4]

The director of Merseyside YPT was (and still is) Paul Harman, who has been with the company since 1970, a fact which represents a considerable degree of continuity. This being so, it is perhaps fortunate that Harman has a fairly catholic taste in plays and does not share the dismissive attitude towards the non-political, 'entertainment' companies which have an undoubted appeal to a large section of the child-audience. Sometimes a TIE company may have a venue of its own (Cockpit); sometimes it may be a touring company confining itself to schools and community centres. Some companies have broadened their appeal and taken on 'community' drama. This involves work for both young people and adults, allowing the actors to extend and redeploy their skills in a way that would gladden the heart of Moses Goldberg who is committed to the idea of the interchange of actors.

Adult drama in this context does not merely mean plays on local themes; thus, Nottingham Playhouse TIE Company could put on a splendid production of Middleton's *Women Beware Women* with a boldness that reminds one of the formal experiments of good TIE work. (Silent film techniques were used to cope with the cumbersome denouement, for example.)

Theatre Centre has a base in Islington and employs three teams, two of which tour schools on a national basis while the third works in Islington itself. When David Johnston left in 1986, after ten years in the driving seat, the advert in the *Guardian* for his successor said: 'Theatre

Centre is committed to feminism and radical social change. We are a multi-racial company and positively welcome all applicants irrespective of race, gender, sexual orientation or physical disability.' Theatre Centre overtly discriminates in favour of disadvantaged groups for all artistic jobs. It is no accident that one of their paymasters was the Greater London Council.

Other companies, however, are also practising 'positive discrimination'. A black delegate at a conference on script-writing denounced all discrimination as 'negative'. There may be good reasons for saying that, all things being equal, a black actor is more appropriate for a particular part than a white one – and vice versa. But for the sake of artistic standards, there ought to be an artistic element in the measurement of appropriateness. Theatre Centre tends to make coloured actors available for non-coloured parts and one is reminded of the current debate in the world of 'adult' theatre about the possibilities of a black or female Hamlet. A review, in the *Guardian* of 22 June 1987 of *A Midsummer Night's Dream* at Nottingham Playhouse, applauded the casting of a black man and woman on account of the appropriateness of the West Indian father–daughter relationship. Kenneth Alan Taylor, the director, made this comment:

> I must confess to being surprised that after all the work that has gone into equal opportunities for black actors and increasingly widespread appearance of black actors, you were unable to evaluate the performances of our black actors on the basis of their abilities rather than their colour. Black actors will continue to appear in classical plays at this theatre and I trust that in future your reviewer will not feel it necessary to find some arcane academic justification for their presence.

The convention will obviously need to become established, and meanwhile directors will have to be vigilant when they attempt to predict what meanings the audience, young or old, will attach to what they see and be scrupulous in according priority to artistic considerations.

Companies organised along hierarchical lines, whether subsidised or 'commercial' were also making their sometimes token, sometimes substantial contribution to theatre for the young. National and regional reps put on main house productions, mainly at Christmas but sometimes in early autumn or summer. Peter Hall, Director of the National Theatre, apologised (in the *Guardian*, 7 January 1987) for the limited scope of his theatre's commitment and made the standard excuse:

> We do a play a year for young people; really we ought to be doing three or four. Instead of giving one hundred performances we should be doing three hundred. We can't afford to; that, of course, is the other thing about children's theatre. It can never be economic because you cannot charge full cost.

There were some notable productions at the National Theatre, though, and the crowning achievement, *Hiawatha* (to be discussed later), was taken on tour as well as being given its first airing in the Olivier auditorium.

The specialist children's theatres with a home base, Unicorn and Polka, fought to fill their auditoriums all the year round. Under Nick Barter, the Arts Theatre at Great Newport Street underwent some radical structural alterations, extending the stage to be nearer to the audience, pulling the circle forward and redesigning the foyer. In 1983, the company of seven actors was putting on five main house productions and there were three studio productions as well per annum. A Unicorn Club was flourising. School parties were encouraged and there was some touring of schools and the obligatory teachers' notes to sell the shows as educationally respectable. Barter himself has a leaning towards the 'sense of occasion' that a visit to an actual theatre can bestow on the youngsters. The target age range was 0–12, but within that band there were shows specially tailored to varying levels of maturity and sophistication. Barter believes there has to be some adjustment for children in terms of language and convention. He had discovered through bitter experience that taking down the lights did not produce in them the expectant hush that falls on an adult audience but acted as a signal for the temperature and volume to rise. He also found that 'the kind of adult drama where two people sit down and talk turns the kids off. It reminds them of excluding parents.' Interviewed in 1983, Barter said his aim was to give the children 'something to think about'. He subscribed, he said, to the nineteenth-century dictum 'to interest, to instruct and occasionally to amuse'. He believed in taking the kids as seriously as adults but conceded that there was still the stigma of lower status about the work for children in the eyes of fellow professionals in the theatre at large.

Barter has tried to offer a varied diet which might include the sort of concerns a TIE company might take on board, but will also represent the interests of non-issue-based writing, if it be of respectable quality. Themes tackled have included loneliness, unpopularity, growing up, the arbitrariness of adults, being ousted by new siblings and death. To help sort out the grain from the never-ending supply of chaff that comes unsolicited (about pixies, gnomes and furry animals), Adrian Mitchell served as Dramaturg as well as resident writer, but other writers of note have contributed to raising the status of the Unicorn's work. They include David Rudkin, Alan Ayckbourn, Joan Aiken, Helen Cresswell, Susan Hill, Ken Campbell and Henry Livings. Nick Barter was also introduced to the work of GRIPS, the West German young people's theatre group, translated by Roy Kift and geared towards helping youngsters face the battles of life. Actors need some adult work to sense the direction in which acting for children could extend, and there needs to be some personal satisfaction and growth both for actors and writers addressing the young. There may be no Hamlet as yet to make a children's play the goal of ambitious top-flight actors, but Barter believed that at least some of his scripts could stretch them.

Unicorn also became the home base in this country for ASSITEJ – the international association of young people's theatre. It operated as an information bureau of a kind, helping foreign visitors, for instance, to know what was going on and directing them to where their interest lay. It could also entertain visiting companies from abroad.

The other specialist children's theatre with a home base in London, Polka, got into its stride under the continuing leadership of Richard Gill and his wife. Gill was himself the author of a number of plays for children and he firmly supported the notion of the author/director – where this was possible. Gill was very articulate on the subject of his philosophy. Like Nick Barter, he believed in the value of a place for children to come to and his preferred size of audience was 300–400. The physical appearance of the 'Enchanted Theatre' made a powerful visual statement about the kind of impact the plays would aim to make. This is all of a piece with Gill's commitment to the importance of visually stunning set design. In the beautifully produced brochures and in interviews, Gill made free use of expressions such as 'magic', 'enrichment' and 'High Art'. The first brochure, issued shortly after the opening, was aggressively assertive as if Gill felt that he had to demolish the pretensions of an existing – figurative – edifice, that of TIE/YPT. While at the same time acknowledging the claim to respectability that an 'educational' justification bestowed, Gill had his own romantic view of what children's theatre ought to do.

> A good children's play is the quickest way – bar none – of getting information into a child's head. Why else should it be so widely used in propaganda? Polka is entirely non-political and we avoid completely all material that is not basically enriching. A vapid fairy story can obviously offer a child nothing but what of our production of *The Odyssey* for children 8–13? In 90 minutes, the audience absorbs and enjoys the whole of Homer's story: it hears real Greek music; it sees authentic costumes, weapons and armour; it sees the gods in action; it learns the geography of the Aegean; it sees Greek architecture – all effortlessly, deeply and quickly.[5]

What price the imaginative truth of the deeds and interactions of human beings? What price metaphor? The same statement was reprinted when the brochure was revised in 1983, but, interestingly, the following was not. It begins with a claim that TIE companies could happily endorse:

> We believe that Children's Theatre is crucial to the mental and spiritual development of children. It is not just 'entertainment' any more than Play is 'just playing' or Craft is 'mucking about with glue'.

Then came the bludgeon:

> Of course it can be abused – by political propaganda on the one hand and by worthless commercial enterprise on the other. Both are equally damaging to the minds of children. But at its best, Children's Theatre is one of the most potent forces in education.
>
> Children's Theatre is a tool of immense power. It must not be used for political propaganda, however oblique. Yes, we have seen an audience-participation show called 'Let's Make a Strike' in Britain in recent years. Proponents of political theatre for children will always tell you that 'of course the children are allowed to make up their own minds'. This is untrue. Children have no intellectual defences against propaganda – and propaganda from the stage works subliminally anyway. They will also say 'It is important for our children to understand social problems of today'. So it is – but in any sort of show, it is impossible to present these problems without bias. That bias is extremely dangerous.[6]

In conversation with me in 1983, David Johnston of Theatre Centre gave it as his opinion that theatres such as Polka, which eschewed (overtly) the political were themselves political by implication, endorsing the status quo. When Roger Jerome interviewed Gill,[7] Gill claimed to offer 'a vast range of different sorts of play'. Many of the presentations were puppet shows or a mixture of puppets and live actors, but there were shows that fall within the scope of this book as well, those put on by professional companies of live actors for young audiences. In the same interview, Jerome says of Gill: 'The enrichment he seeks should contain elements of life at present, the magic carpet doesn't stay aloft for ever.' There was a rumour that one of the paymasters (the Arts Council?) had leaned on Polka to embrace the 'social realist' as well as the fantastic. In the 1983 brochure, Gill records the programme for the preceding twelve months under the heading 'A Year at the Children's Theatre'.

TREASURE ISLAND: Drama for 7–13s by Richard Gill, after Robert Louis Stevenson.

TOWN MOUSE, COUNTRY MOUSE: Comedy for 4–6s by Vicky Ireland.

THE WONDERFUL LAMP: Drama with magic for 5–500s by Richard Gill.

PIERO PLAYS HIS PART: Mime play for 5–8s by Peri Aston.

SMASH AND GRAB: Black-Theatre Puppet Spectacle for 7–11s by Marjanka Vrabcove.

ALL IN STITCHES: Sociological comedy for 5–8s by Veit/Ludwig/Kift.

TUTANKAMUN: Documentary drama with fabulous replicas and puppets for 7–adult by Nick Read.

THE WIND IN THE WILLOWS: Marionette play for 6–10s by Kenneth Grahame.

It is interesting how sure Gill is that he can hit an age-band with such accuracy. The token 'social realist' offering, *All in Stitches*, an import from GRIPS, was set in a children's ward in a hospital where it busied itself with brushing aside young patients' fears. We shall be discussing a performance of it later.

David Wood subscribes to the philosophy of Richard Gill with regard to the importance of physical context. He, too, wants to produce in his young audiences a 'gasp of wonder'. Whirligig, his company, though, is a touring company *tout simple*. The sets which trigger off the 'wonder', are erected afresh in a succession of established metropolitan and provincial theatres. Unlike the Christmas pantomimes, which it was once Wood's ambition to replace, Whirligig can perform at all times of the year.

When he first began his activities in the 1970s, Wood's venture was purely commercial, but he soon admitted the vital need for sponsorship. Arts Council money was slow to come, but in 1983 he was in receipt of £45,000 towards the cost of a twelve-week run of *The Selfish Shellfish*. Clarke's Shoes came in with a subsidy but Wood could never allow himself to sit back and trust to the continuing bounty of his patrons. He works from his home in Wimbledon and he and Jack Gould do all the administration between them.

David Wood is very much in charge of his operation and even the dramatic material he purveys is largely his own creation. He has a penchant for musicals and he also writes the tunes and lyrics in styles varying from rock to soul. He is on record as having said he would consider scripts by other authors but they will have to suit the 'house style'. He tries to engage reputable actors when possible, which is consistent with his policy of raising the status of children's theatre all round. Like Gill, Wood invokes educational benefit as one justification of his work, thinking largely in terms of 'creative' follow-up projects that teachers could launch, but his plays are complete experiences in themselves. He sides with Gill in his nervousness of the political propaganda that some TIE groups appear to indulge in. Nevertheless, despite his overriding commitment to 'entertainment', Wood has, like Richard Gill, swum a little way with the tide and introduced social themes into his plays. In Whirligig's 'Press Information', *The Selfish Shellfish* is described as tackling a 'contemporary ecological problem'. Generally, though, the experience of a Wood play is not a very disturbing one deep down and he has not received the accolade of being censored. The plots follow a pattern, a formula. 'The story involves a predicament, complicated by the malfaisance of a villain who gets a (mild) come-uppance.'[8] He aims for pace, clarity and sincerity. He is a very moral writer ('His recipes are full of warm goodness', *The Stage*) and justice is done, justice being what Wood believes children find most satisfying.

In the 1980s, David Wood has been a much and widely produced writer, both at home and abroad. His plays have been taken over by provincial repertory companies and in venues like the Young Vic. *The Gingerbread Man* has an almost classic status. Wood's plays have been published, mainly by Samuel French. He has done his no small best to raise the standing of children's threatre and is to be applauded for his seriousness. The settings of his stories have a freshness of conception and the words try to avoid the banal. He still uses the pantomime paraphernalia of audience participation but not without achieving some contact through his central vision. He does fill houses, too. Certain TIE/YPT companies outclass him by their experiments with form and the portentousness of their subject matter, but they sometimes lack his instinct for the grabbing and holding of attention.

4
Fantasy in a Traditional Mould

In this, and in the next three chapters, we come to a more detailed consideration of particular plays and, where possible, of these plays as events. Some have been published and although I have not seen them on stage, I can comment on their theatrical potential and other people's observations of them in action. Performances for children have not always been given the journalistic attention they are worth but there has been some improvement in their status of late. For some plays a typescript has been available and typescripts do sometimes get passed around the companies. Again, I have been able to lay my hands on a number of these. There are other plays which were never written down and existed only in performance. Since I did not start systematically recording events until the 1980s, my accounts of performances are necessarily confined to plays which either originated in or survived into the present decade.

I have not, then, tried to give an exhaustive survey of the cultural phenomenon of theatre for the young in Great

1. *The Gingerbread Man* by David Wood; Designer: Susie Caulcutt (photograph © Laurence Burns).

Britain. I have chosen examples which represent the range of style and preoccupation of the originators. They also, in my view, span a range of artistic quality. But while paying tribute to those which are truly significant, I have taken as my main concern the testing and establishment of valid criteria that one is entitled to apply to the pieces. The sort of questions I have asked myself (selected according to the context) are as follows:

- Has the play/performance got the simultaneous subjectivity/objectivity of Art?
- Is its imaginative vision convincing? Is it 'true to life'?
- Has it the courage, if necessary, to disturb?
- Is it a satisfying experience in itself, quite apart from any educational spin-off or follow-up to which it might be made to give rise?
- Does it manage to make appropriate allowances for the artistic and intellectual sophistication of the audience without 'writing down' to them? Does it show 'respect' for children?
- Does it observe the right to autonomy on the part of both artists and audience?
- Does it avoid bullying the audience? Do the characters themselves know the 'message'? What is the effect if they do?
- Does the play work in the chosen theatrical venue?
- How effective is its theatrical structure?
- Does it make expressive use of the elements of the theatrical medium, such as word, image and sign?
- Does it use and need song and dance?
- Does it use participation strategies other than the spontaneous? If so, how do they effect the meaningfulness of the experience for the audience?

We look first at some plays which build on traditional stories, nursery rhymes, myths and legends or which make use of traditional-style ingredients and structures. They often create a fantasy world where magic is not just possible but rampant. They may rely on our knowledge and memory of a traditional story to force a change of perspective by frustrating our customary response. At best, they embody truths about human experience; at worst, the fantasy world offers an escape from the real one.

Peter Pan

The most firmly established play of this kind in Britain, and the one which, by dint of its long-term popularity, might qualify to be described as a 'classic', is *Peter Pan*. Perversely, it was not aimed at children but at the child in all of us, and it so happened that at its first production audiences were largely adult. For most theatres that put it on, though, it counts as their children's show, or as one of their children's shows. Since December 1904, when it was first produced at the Duke of York's Theatre by American impresario Charles Frohman, *Peter Pan* was produced annually up to the beginning of World War Two and then from 1940 without interruption until 1969. Then it lapsed in 1970, 1976, 1980 and 1981. There were voices to say that the play was losing its grip at last, but some of the revivals in the 1980s have proved its continuing appeal and given a new vitality to it.

The story begins in the night nursery of the Darling household in a shabby-genteel part of Bloomsbury where live Mr and Mrs Darling, their children Wendy, John and Michael, Liza the maid, and Nana the nurse, who is also a Newfoundland dog. A boy has appeared to Mrs Darling, floating outside the window, and Nana, giving chase, has trapped the boy's shadow. Mr and Mrs Darling are about to go out to a dinner party, but father is irritable and he becomes jealous of Nana's status in the household and chains her up. When the parents have gone out, Peter returns for his shadow with Tinkerbell, a fairy. Interrupted by Wendy, who is awakened, he tells Wendy all about himself; how he lost his mother, how he lives in the Neverland and how he looks after the Lost Boys. The Lost Boys, as Peter says, 'are the children who fall out of their prams when the nurse is looking the other way. If they are not claimed in seven days they are sent far away to the Neverland.' He tries to entice Wendy and her brothers to come, so that Wendy can take on the role of mother. He teaches them all to fly. They go and the Darling parents are broken hearted.

In Neverland, the Lost Boys, Tootles, Nibs, Slightly, Curly and the twins await the return of Peter. We are introduced to Captain Hook, whose arm was cut off by Peter and fed to a crocodile that now pursues Hook to eat the rest of him but is handicapped by the loud ticking of a clock it has swallowed, thus warning off its victim. We also see another faction at war with the pirates, the Red Indians. Tinkerbell arrives and, out of jealousy for Wendy, tells the boys that Peter wants them to shoot down the Wendy bird when she flies in. Tootles does so. Peter returns and is furious and concerned. He orders a house to be built around Wendy. Michael and John also arrive in the Neverland.

The action moves to the mermaids' lagoon, where the pirates, having captured Tiger Lily, the Indian leader, deposit her on a rock. Peter, imitating Hook's voice, orders them to free her. Hook is furious. He tells his men that the boys have found a new mother in Wendy and the pirates want to claim her for their mother, too. Peter and Wendy become marooned on a rock but Peter grabs a kite and encourages Wendy to hang on to it and float away. He claims it won't take two, and, ever the gentleman, he gives priority to the lady. A stage direction assures us that Peter could go if he wanted to, since he is weightless, but he prefers to relish the thought of death, as 'an awfully big adventure'. Nevertheless he leaps on a passing bird's nest and sails home.

Home is, in fact, underground. The redskins are above, now sworn to eternal friendship with Peter. He plays father, and Wendy, as mother, tells her 'children' about her and her brothers' real home. Peter is moved to express his sadness at the loss of his own mother, who replaced him with another boy after giving him up for lost. There is talk of going back to the Darlings' house and only Peter refuses the prospect of adoption. A fight occurs between pirates and redskins. Peter thinks the redskins have won and he goes to sleep. But Hook sneaks down and poisons Peter's medicine. In an access of self-sacrifice, Tinkerbell drinks it and Peter exhorts the audience to revive her by clapping.

The boys and Wendy, meanwhile, have all been captured by the pirates and are condemned to walk the plank. John and Michael are offered the alternative of acting as cabin-boys but, being true Brits, they refuse. Peter lures the pirates one by one into a cabin by intriguing them with the noise of a cock-a-doodle-doo. Desperately, Hook proposes to throw the 'unlucky' Wendy overboard but Peter reveals himself and, on behalf of joy and youth, challenges Hook. Hook threatens to blow up the ship but the crocodile finally gets him and, not unheroically and singing 'Floreat Etona', Hook goes to his death.

In the nursery, at the Darling household, the window

remains hopefully open. Father is punishing himself by living, literally, in the doghouse. The children return, to mother's delight, and the Darlings adopt all the boys except Slightly, who is adopted by his true mother, Liza, and Peter, who still refuses. Mother will not let Wendy go away again just now so Peter has to settle for an annual visit from Wendy to spring-clean. Wendy will, of course, grow up, but Peter will be boy eternal.

By general agreement – even Barrie's – the author of *Peter Pan* invested a lot of himself in his creation, based his fiction on his own experience and acquaintances, and expressed in it strong personal feelings. The relationship between a boy and his mother is a central preoccupation in much of Barrie's writing, seen also in his novels and other plays. Barrie's elder brother died just before his fourteenth birthday and Barrie tried to insinuate himself into the dead boy's place. His failure to do so aroused powerful and persistent feelings of rejection and jealousy. In manhood, he befriended the Llewellyn-Davies boys, who, according to Barrie, furnished him with a composite hero in Peter, while their mother may, in some ways, have contributed to Mrs Darling. Barrie, in fact, became the children's guardian when their parents died, his own failed marriage having proved childless.

Using one's own experience as a springboard is not, in itself, turning a play into an excuse for self-indulgence. Unless a writer cares about his characters, he cannot expect the audience to care. The act of creating a fiction can be a learning experience for a writer in which he achieves new perspectives on familiar territory. He can thus make it possible for an audience to 'grow' too.

Much of the criticism of Barrie has maintained that he learned nothing, that his hang-ups were too powerful to overcome and that his creativity was blighted in the bud.

Peter Coveney finds in *Peter Pan* a retreat from adult responsibility, an unredeemed nostalgia for childhood to which both writers and audience were susceptible at the turn of the century. They would have echoed De La Mare's *cri de coeur*:

> What can the tired heart say,
> That the wise of the world have made dumb,
> Save to the lonely dreams of a child
> Return again, come?

Coveney says:

> Just as it is important to distinguish true art from distracting biographical entanglements, it is none the less important to disentangle the idea of art from the meretricious products which are the exact expression of an author's sickness. It is the very power of Barrie's 'complex' which gives the undeniable but nevertheless debilitating power to his writing.[1]

According to Coveney, Mrs Darling is one example of a sickly glorification of motherhood. For her, the night-lights she leaves at bed time are 'the eyes a mother leaves behind to guard her children'. Such examples of the twee and the precious are unfortunately not rare in the piece. Is Peter the idealised hero and is he enviable? Certainly Neverland offers the thrill of adventure to appeal to the child in all of us. But there is something potentially chilling in Peter which the play seems to recognise or at least what modern productions have successfully brought out. He is self-centred, callous and mischievous, a fighter who can cut off arms and systematically do in a succession of pirates. He is a poseur and exhibitionist, embracing the notion of death as an 'awfully big adventure', in the knowledge that he can escape if he really wants to. In the end, when he finds himself alone and unadopted, he does not indulge in self-pity. Barrie says he has the 'devil' in him. Prompted by Barrie's own retrospective comment (in a note book) it is not unusual now for critics (and directors like Trevor Nunn) to talk of the 'tragedy' of Peter, the boy who makes 'a desperate attempt to grow up, but can't'. As Huckleberry Finn did in fleeing from 'sivilisation', Peter rejects the 'success' and conformity demanded by the society of adults:

> PETER: Would you send me to school?
> MRS DARLING: Yes.
> PETER: And then to office?
> MRS DARLING: I suppose.
> PETER: Soon I should be a man?
> MRS DARLING: Very soon.
> PETER: [Passionately] I don't want to go to school and learn solemn things. No one is going to catch me, lady and make me a man. I want always to be a little boy and have fun.

The resemblance to Huck Finn stops there, though. Huck's childlike innocence affords him insights that the adult world would do well to act upon. Peter is not destroyed by his own flaws or crushed by fate. We are not overwhelmed with a sense of waste. It is a moot point whether Peter shows the desperation to grow up. Possibly his situation is pitiable but it is not pity that Peter begs for.

The central relationship of the play is not between Peter and Mrs Darling, of course, but between Peter and Wendy. At one point, Peter plays father and mother with her, but it is only in a game that he can do so. One does not sense any Freudian eroticism. They have a strong attachment but it is pre-pubescent.

> WENDY: What are your exact feelings for me, Peter?
> PETER: Those of a devoted son, Wendy;

Between Wendy and Tinkerbell, though, there is something approaching sexual jealousy; and in the role of mother, Wendy can be bossy and possessive when she wants to.

The play deals with serious enough themes, such as the nature and importance of the parent–child relationship and of family life, and death occurs and is contemplated. There is, however, apart from sentimentality, a pervading humour which is sometimes enlightening, sometimes whimsical and trivialising. Potentially, I should add, since there does seem to be legitimate choice as to how to interpret and realise the play. When Peter makes his vacuous statement about death being an awfully big adventure, it is the stage direction that tells us he *could* escape if he so desired. In performance, the pose could be shown as being more difficult for Peter to strike. His heroic pronouncement when he challenges Hook ('Put up your swords, boys. This man is mine.') could be 'sent up' without violating the tone. Hook himself is a semi-comic figure who dies with 'Floreat Etona' on his lips. It is interesting that, in performance, the part of Hook is usually doubled up with that of Mr Darling, which says something about the status of father, possibly. Mr Darling castigates himself for his overbearing attitude and carries a dog kennel around with him as punishment, an image worthy of N. F. Simpson and the theatre of the absurd. Hook can be frightening, though, in the theatre, which is more than can be said of the pirates. Barrie claims

Treasure Island as one of his sources, but the real fear Stevenson's pirates inspire and the real significance of death in the novel are of a different order. Death puts into perspective the greed for gold of both Silver and his gang and the Squire and his faction. Jim Hawkins has an awfully big adventure but the issues are truly serious. Barrie's pirates owe more to Gilbert and Sullivan than to Stevenson. One cannot imagine the wickedness of Israel Hands being neutralised by the acquisition of a mother.

We have said that Peter questions the satisfaction offered by the kinds of work available in a particular society, but, on the whole, the play implicitly seems to endorse the society of which it writes. Though shabby-genteel, the Darlings must have a nanny to look after the children. There is an emphasis on patriotism and heroic sacrifices for King and Country. Peter acts according to good form, and Hook's pride in his old public school could partly be meant to redeem him. One is reminded of another of Barrie's plays, *The Admirable Crichton*, in which Barrie questions the validity of the traditional hierarchical society on a desert island, only to deny, in the end, that there are grounds for destroying it in England. There is no political examination of the status of women: Wendy happily accepts her domestic responsibilities as a mother while the boys are not having adventures and fun.

Such, then seem to be the parameters of meaning and interpretation the script alone offers the reader. But it is important to our thesis that events in a theatre, the human action in a particular setting, add up to a unique experience, and the play ought, if possible, to be judged in that light. The 1904 production created certain precedents, the most important of which was that Peter should be played by a woman, like the principal boy in a pantomime. Barrie himself wanted Gerald du Maurier to play the part but instead got Nina Boucicault. The audience contained a goodly proportion of adults who dutifully clapped to revive Tinkerbell and these adults were on hand to assuage the children's fear of Captain Hook.

The performance of 'Peter Pan' at the Crucible Theatre, Sheffield, by the Crucible Company, December 1982

The production at the Crucible Theatre, Sheffield, in 1982, was content to follow established lines. Peter was played by an actress, Paula Wilcox, in the recommended costume of autumn leaves and cobwebs. She was cool but she softened the 'masculine' side of the character, or had it softened for her, by the fact that the lost boys were played by adult men. This despite the fact that the actors captured the gaucheness of children with unpatronising conviction. Peter did accept the loss of Wendy at first almost indifferently but his later separation was moving and full of regrets.

Wendy (Joanne Whalley) was described by a reviewer of this production as: 'appealing in a winsome, pre-Raphaelite way – a soft-focus woodland nymph in a blue velvet cloak with red berries picturesquely fastening the hem of her white nightdress above pearly ankles, the virgin Wendy, distant but infinitely compassionate and tender'.[2] Mrs Darling was similarly pretty and Mr Darling good on the comic dimension. As Captain Hook, Bryan Pringle was hardly frightening at all. Clare Venables, the director, told me Mr Pringle was constitutionally incapable of being nasty, so we have to accept and build on what he does have to offer. Presumably, though, someone cast him . . . Irene McManus dubbed the production 'feminine'. It was certainly romantic and dreamlike in style but there was also a deliberate gentleness. Clare

Venables did not believe in frightening children in the theatre and, as a mother herself, instinctively found herself trying to protect them. A further air of unreality was created by the stylised way the characters delivered their lines. Mrs Darling was not allowed to communicate fear of the marauding Peter at the beginning. The fight between the boys and the pirates was emasculated by using pillows as weapons. With such cuddly pirates, it was difficult to accept the narrative fact that they were all killed later – and by Peter Pan.

The director did seize opportunities for comedy that the play makes available. Sometimes this had the effect of drawing the sting but at others it afforded sardonic perspectives. If Father's withdrawal to the doghouse was funny, so was the way he secretely enjoyed this martyrdom. Skilfully-used music had the effect of toning down unwanted laughter. Plangent Sibelius inhibited mockery at the notion of the detachable shadow, and Beethoven later dignified the sad figure of Mrs Darling at her endless vigil for her returning young.

The performance took place on the Crucible's main house thrust stage. This brings players to audience in a manner Brian Way might approve of. The trouble is that, in a play that thrives on magical illusions, the Crucible can ruthlessly demystify. The 'flying' mechanism was too crude to youngsters who had seen Superman fly on film without slips or wires. The crocodile was just cute and various feathered properties evoked knowing comments such as: 'Hey, look at that duck. It's plastic!' But when, upstage, the gauze trapping an orange glow opened to reveal the clean, almost sterilised Darling home, the effect was breathtaking.

The audience when I saw the production had a fairly large sprinkling of adults, but when they clapped for

Tinkerbell it seemed a token response. I certainly did not get the impression that belief in fairies was being passionately asserted or that the adults were on a simple nostalgia jag or that the kids were a slave to daydream.

The performance of 'Peter Pan' at the Barbican, London, by the Royal Shakespeare Company, 23 December 1982

By contrast with the Crucible production of *Peter Pan*, 1982 also saw the launching of a revolutionary version by the RSC at the Barbican. Being the RSC's, the event excited much interest in the press and attracted capacity audiences. Trevor Nunn, one of the play's directors, pronounced it a 'neglected masterpiece', which he admitted sounded strange considering it had had more productions than any other play this century.[3] Michael Billington endorsed its status, since not only did it show the 'tragic' dilemma of a boy faced with two undesirable alternatives, but 'simultaneously taps the age-old hunger for adventure, flight and romance'.[4]

The new production lasted three hours and incorporated not merely the 1904 text but excerpts from the 1911 novel and the 1920 film version, and also the *Afterthought*, an episode last performed in 1908. The *Afterthought* features the children grown-up and underlines the play's tragic potential by showing Peter failing to persuade Wendy to go spring-cleaning as she has a daughter of her own now.

The most noteworthy innovation was the casting of a man as Peter; Miles Anderson in the first instance but Mark Rylance when I saw it. Robert Cushman thought that 'there was not much in Peter for a grown up male actor to act'.[5] Heather Neill thought Rylance 'added a welcome strangeness, an other-worldliness' and was of the opinion that the part was a challenge to the actor.[6] Mr Cushman is right that in Peter we have not yet found the children's Hamlet, but there is more complexity and there are more contradictions than was traditionally believed. Peter now becomes a descendant of Puck, a reminder of the ragged boy Heathcliffe. He is a strutting macho male who, sadly, cannot relate to a real mother. In the production under discussion, there was now something faintly erotic about Peter's relationship with Wendy, and the new Wendy shows real sexual jealousy of Tinkerbell. Death, for this Peter, was something he had to square himself to face. In the end, the soaring, spectacular flying that this theatre made possible gave up an image of Peter triumphant – or at least feeling triumphant. The sweet Darling ménage was predictably cloying, but this time it almost seemed as if Barrie knew it too; that it was, in Cushman's words, 'simultaneously loathed and desired by its creator'.[7]

Another innovation was the introduction of a Narrator. Sometimes he clarified, sometimes he destroyed ('It's awfully sad, isn't it?' Wait for laugh), sometimes he was just unnecessary. Possibly an import from the RSC's *Nicholas Nickleby*, he spelt out the issues, distanced us from the action (for example with a joke about there being a discrepancy between his watch and the croc's alarm clock), interpreted for us, covered scene changes (always a problem with this demanding piece) and made use of material usually confined to stage directions. He pointed out that there was 'one joy from which Peter must be forever barred' and his comment on Peter's loss of his mother was very moving. Introducing the pirates one by one was a waste of time as it did not help us remember them, but reminding us who the (changed) grown-up boys were at the end made an ironic point – how changed they in fact were.

Hook still failed to frighten us but his lines never did help much and can effectively castrate the actor. The crocodile, though, transcended the pantomimic. Cushman avers that 'something it signally lacks compared with the fantasy classics is laughter'.[8] By 'fantasy classics' he means the work of Lewis Carroll, Kenneth Grahame and A. A. Milne. But one can never be so categorical about a play and I found the performance I saw contained more comedy than the Crucible one. There was laughter at the Darlings; not just at the Father but at Michael crying and at Tootles shooting Wendy. The adults in the audience started hissing at the appearance of Hook, thus attempting to reduce something new to the manageability of the customary.

John Napier's setting in this huge auditorium has been described (by Michael Billington) as a 'semi-surreal adventure playground'. There were vivid effects such as the stretched blue canvas that created the sea. Music by Stephen Oliver (of *Nicholas Nickleby* fame) simply but effectively accompanied the feats of action.

Pinocchio

The choice between growing up and having fun faces another character well known in children's theatre circles, Pinocchio. Talking of Pinocchio brings us to the phenomenon of the adaptor, since all performance versions of the story trace their origins to the book by Carlo Collodi. How far is the adaptor duty-bound to reproduce the precise patterns of attraction and the value systems of the original? From my experience as an adaptor of children's books for television and for the stage, I would say that one cannot claim to have adapted a book at all unless one has shown some sympathy for what it is saying and implying. But it is also true that the adaptor is not transparent, however faithful he attempts to be, and that anything filtered through him will involve changes of meaning. One has to judge a stage artefact as a play in its own right.

Briefly, the story of Pinocchio is the story of a wooden puppet, made by an old man, Gepetto, which comes to life. The moment it does so, it becomes rebellious, impertinent and violent. A talking cricket gives him moral advice but Pinocchio throws a mallet at the insect and kills him. Gepetto wants Pinocchio to go to school with the object of his becoming a real boy, but, despite his promises, Pinocchio is tempted by the life of adventure, fun and self-indulgence. He is beguiled by a marionette show presided over by a 'tall and ugly' Showman, who threatens to chop him up for firewood, but, on learning that Pinocchio is a product of his old friend Gepetto, he gives the puppet five gold pieces for his 'father'. On his way home, Pinocchio is waylaid by a Fox and a Cat who tell him he could increase his money if he buried it in the Field of Miracles. Then two 'assassins' try to kill him for his money, hang him from a tree and leave him to die. He is rescued by the minions of a Blue Fairy. He lies about his money to the Fairy and his nose starts to grow. He does visit the Field of Miracles and buries his money but the Cat and the Fox make off with it. After other adventures Pinocchio is shocked to discover the grave of the Blue Fairy, killed, he is told, by reports of his immoral behaviour. She comes back to life, though, and delivers him a sermon. This time he does go to school, but a fellow pupil, Lampwick, tempts him to skip off to Toyland (a kind of Neverland?) where fun is the order of the day. Both youngsters get changed into donkeys. Pinocchio learns that Gepetto has set off in search of him, and he runs away to look for Gepetto. The trail takes him into a boat on the sea, but a shark swallows him, not, however, before the sea has transformed him into marionette again. Lo and behold, inside the shark he meets Gepetto and rescues him. They return home and Pinocchio becomes a real boy. He learns that Lampwick has died.

There is plenty of incident for a playwright to work on and an ambivalent central character with internal and external conflicts. Characters in the book, like the Blue Fairy and the Cricket, indulge in some hefty and stern moralising, preaching the old-fashioned virtues of hard work, study, obedience to parents, telling the truth, keeping promises and 'growing up'. The story does not shrink from violence (committed by or against Pinocchio) and death.

Brian Way opts for a fairly bland and sanitised version. He has this to say: 'Some will notice that the original story by Collodi has not been followed very closely. This is because it is not really a very pleasant story.'[9]

As Aidan Chambers comments: 'There is a gentleness of tone, a public courtesy among the characters and between characters and audience that gives his [i.e. Way's] plays an atmosphere of optimistic, if a little old-worldly, charm by contrast with the brashly abrasive style of younger and more fashionable writings such as Ken Campbell's.'[10] Of Campbell, more anon.

The Fire-Eater, equivalent to Collodi's Showman, is a lovable chap, and all the violence has been toned down: no flattened crickets, no hanging Pinocchios, no fairies dying of disappointment. Lessons are learned (both in school and out of it). Lampwick (Candlewick, in Way) instead of dying is restored to human shape by the fairy.

When Pinocchio becomes a real boy, 'Everyone is astonished. Everyone is happy.'

Pinocchio is the *locus classicus* for the application of Way's theory of audience participation. He claims to want the children to have real influence over the unfolding of the action, but the 'bond' he hopes the actors will form with the audience is often a one-way commitment by the audience to supporting decisions already made by the playwright. Gepetto has always wanted to make a live puppet but the power of his wishing was not strong enough. Perhaps the audience would help:

> I've always wanted to make a puppet that could walk without any strings at all! Yes, yes. Think of it. Me, a poor old man – what fun I'd have! Sometimes, you know, I want it so much that I sit and wish very hard with my eyes shut, like this [he demonstrates] But it doesn't seem to work. I suppose the trouble is that I'm so little that I can't wish big enough. Eh? Could be that, you know. Ooooooh, Ooooooh! wait a minute though. Ooooooh, I, – I don't want to trouble *you*, you know, but – but perhaps you'd like to help. Course nothing might happen – but then again something might – if we wished hard ALL TOGETHER. [whispering] Shall we try it? Shall we? Oh, thank you very much . . .

But the Fairy is going to come and help anyway just as Tinkerbell was going to recover. Later, Pinocchio omits to wash and clean his teeth, so to encourage him the audience is urged to join in. Not a lot of creative response required here. At one point, where it looks possible the children might enjoin Pinocchio to go to school rather than off on the adventure trail, Way gives advice as to how the director might find an alternative path to the play's predictable end:

> It may well happen on occasions that the audience is so concerned with Pinocchio's welfare that they refuse to allow him to talk to Fox and Cat but insist instead that he goes to school. If they do this with some vigour, then there is no point in trying to stick to the next few pages of script. Better by far to let Pinocchio accept the advice and run away with Fox and Cat in pursuit. Pinocchio could then call for the policeman and Fox and Cat hide when he appears – thence into the detective scene.

I know that Way is child-centred in his preferences, but why is it so awful that children should face the fact that they cannot mould the world according to their whims or, since a finished play *is* a world of a kind, the world of the play?

Derby Playhouse decided to put on *Pinocchio* for its 1983 Christmas show but they commissioned a new version from Gary Yershon on the strength of his musical composition for *Cinderella* the previous year. Actors were brought in from the current adult production of *The Ghost Train* to swell the company.

The performance of 'Pinocchio' at Derby Playhouse by the Derby Playhouse Company, 13 December 1983

The writer and the director tried to keep something of the fairy-story appeal while incorporating some of the more shocking and frightening events. The space-age set had a huge kaleidoscopic mirror central which changed the location in conjunction with flown flats and curtains, and the mirror was flanked by leaning scaffolding, up which went crazy catwalks and down which characters could swing on to the stage. The mirror effect started with a spectrum of colours in the centre which fanned outwards. It was particularly effective for the bed of the sleeping Blue Fairy; for the sinister, beckoning Showman, silhouetted and gigantesque and surrounded with smoke; as the Fun Fair where it simulated the succession of neon lights on a roundabout, moving in and out of the centre; and as the inside of the shark's mouth. The shark's teeth glowed in the darkness as did the fluorescent fishes and the octopus. The play was presented on a proscenium stage, and it managed to be stylised and yet to create traditional illusionary, theatrical 'magic' and a sense of wonder. Way recommended an anti-illusionary arena stage. One might think this would enable the young audience to confront the gamut of emotions that *Pinocchio* evokes with more equanimity, but Way was at pains to play down the unpleasant side of experience. In *Development Through Drama*, his educational manifesto, he said that 'drama' may provide 'the only opportunities for experiencing nobler and finer emotions' and that these opportunities should be taken.[11]

'The play could be performed with hats, scarves and other tokens rather than complete costumes', he said.[12] But Chris Honer, Derby's director, gave Pinocchio yellow hair, an orange waistcoat and patch trousers. The Showman's outfit was outrageously voluminous. The Fox had a trilby and his clothes were appropriately red-brown, the Cat in a 'dress' of spotted white. Cricket looked like a cleric or academic, with shaven head, dark-rimmed glasses, black frock cut-away coat and black shiny tights.

The company had the music severval weeks in advance, thus avoiding 'the usual last-minute children's theatre scramble'. Performed by a small band of instrumentalists, it deliberately avoided sugary cadences – perhaps too sedulously, as there was a dearth of memorable or gripping tunes. Disharmonies and minor chords abounded. The overall feel, though, was, at its best, suggestive of Kurt Weill.

At this matinée performance there was a large audience of school parties and youngsters with parents. The performance opened with some jazzy narrative: then Gepetto's puppet came to life. *A la* Brian Way, Gepetto asked the audience to help suggest a name and they were way ahead with 'Pinocchio'. Musical routines were useful in establishing that Pinocchio's mischief was habitual. 'Eat, drink, sleep and play' are the puppet's ambitions and the Cricket, his self-appointed conscience, sang a song which dragged. The kids got very restless, partly, I suspect, becaus the song slowed things up and partly because the kids disliked the preaching. Gepetto urged Pinocchio to 'grow up' and find a place in the world and then tried to bribe him with an apple. What the kids did like was the device of the misheard word –

GEPETTO: I am a fair man . . .
PINOCCHIO: A fair man.
GEPETTO: A kind man . . .
PINOCCHIO: A kind man.
GEPETTO: A just man.
PINOCCHIO: A dustman.
GEPETTO: No, not a dustman, a just man.

A laugh at the expense of one sanctimonious Gepetto! They also enjoyed the send-up of the Fox's pompous language as the Cat, in like manner, undercut him.

CAT: I'm starving. What we gonna do about something to eat?

FOX: Ah, yes, sustenance. That would certainly be extremely pleasant. But sadly we are impecunious and impoverished, insufficient and insolvent, under nourished, underprivileged . . .

CAT: And broke.

FOX: That as well.

The two villains, by the way, entered from the back of the auditorium, thus breaking the tyranny of the proscenium arch. Unfortunately, when they entered, they launched into a song declaring their intentions and describing their practice. The words were difficult to catch and attend to, and the kids responded with renewed restlessness. Words alone would have worked better. When Pinocchio addressed the audience direct with, 'Shall I go to school or shall I go to the puppet show?' they were vehemently split and the play continued on its own sweet way.

Scene changes involved a descending curtain but they were neatly done. The Harlequinade characters came into the story as puppets and with them a good song: 'Puppets never grow up'. The Showman made a terrifying entrance with his whip, but on learning that Pinocchio was the 'child' of his old friend Gepetto, his mild side took over and he gave him five gold pieces for the old puppet-master. The Cricket came in promptly with a timely moral: 'The only people who get rich quick are gamblers and crooks.' Despite the Kurt Weill feel to the music, the 'Song of the Stone' was a signal for more turbulence among the spectators.

On the appeal from Pinocchio, the attention was recaptured. 'Shall I go straight home or go to the Field of

Miracles?' he asked. 'Go straight home!' urged his listeners. 'I'll go straight home – later', said Pinocchio, nothing abashed. The mirror did its spectacular changes to quick-rhythm music and a Brian Way-chase took place involving the Cat and the Fox. They caught Pinocchio and hung him up on the scaffolding where a spotlight transfixed him in a most disturbing image. The Blue Fairy stepped out of the mirror in a magical rescue and sang a tediously righteous song: 'When someone you love lets you down'.

After the interval, Pinocchio confessed he had lost the money (dug up by the Cat) and he wept with remorse at the 'let down' Fairy's sufferings. Pinocchio's behaviour had literally made her sick. 'Shall I go to school?' he asked the audience. 'Yes!' replied some; 'No' the others. So we went, as arranged! There was a scene in school, and school seemed so boring that even its former supporters among the audience defected in droves when Pinocchio asked for guidance on whether he should go with a fellow pupil, Lampwick, to Funland or stay in the boring educational institution. Once again the puppet succumbed to temptation despite the fact that a song urged him to 'Think!' The Showman pre-empted any 'thinking' with a spectacular entrance reflected in the mirrors. A song about 'Paradise' fell on many impatient and unresponsive ears in the audience. In Funland, people became donkeys and the shark scene worked its visual spell as Pinocchio and Gepetto were (chorally) reunited. Harlequin and his associates had set up a workers' co-operative. Fox and Cat had a comic stylised fight, and when they kissed and made up it set the audience whistling. Pinocchio became, according to the Fairy, 'a naughty but nice, honest-to-goodness, real live boy' (played by a girl, to reverse the Peter Pan trend). Lampwick died!

The production tried to emphasise the moral implications of the story while trying to avoid being nauseating. The moralistic songs, though, were often counter-productive. In the interests of dramatic balance and credibility, school was shown as boring by comparison with Funland. But we were shown the sinister side of the tempting Showman, and the kids were genuinely divided in their advice. Fox and Cat were rapacious and violent, it is true, but in this production they almost seemed like the weak side of Pinocchio's character.

One of the best-known stories of talking animals is *Wind in the Willows* by Kenneth Grahame and the most famous stage adaptation of this work that of A. A. Milne. The story charts the adventures of the flamboyant, craze-following Mr Toad and his long-suffering companions, Mole, Rat and Badger. These characters are carefully individualised but are all lovable, and the villains, the Wild Wooders, are easily recognisable as such, since they acquire property which is not theirs, that is Toad Hall. They are eventually brought to heel, however, and Toad promises to reform. Milne treats the subject with a saving humour and with some rousing songs, but a new version I saw in New York in 1983 presented the leading four as indistinguishable and substituted its own saccharine melodies. One has a certain sympathy with the director of the Milne version several years ago at the Sheffield Crucible, where the four heroes were dressed as Edwardian gentlemen and the Wild Wooders shown in their true colours as members of the working class. A refreshing tilt of the balance.

The film version of L. Frank Baum's novel *The Wizard of Oz* is probably better known than the book, and the new adaptor faces a formidable challenge – how to avoid cashing in on existing expectations. Alfred Bradley made a creditable attempt. As Chambers says: 'Bradley's adaptation not only retains Baum's innocent quality but provides opportunities for productions either of a very simple or a very elaborate kind.'[13] But in 1987, the Royal Shakespeare Company, no less, launched an adaptation by John Kane which unashamedly reproduced the wish-fulfilment atmosphere of the film in a spectacular setting. In its publicity handout, it says:

> Nothing can match the magic of this fabulous musical. With a terrific score which includes such unforgettable classics as 'We're off to see the Wizard' and 'Follow the Yellow Brick Road', and of course with Judy Garland captivating with 'Over the Rainbow', the film of *The Wizard of Oz* has been an all time favourite. It is a wonderful mixture of musical fantasy and comedy, following the adventures of Dorothy Gale as she is blown by a cyclone from Kansas to the Land of Oz and makes her way to the Emerald City with her bizarre companions, the Scarecrow, the Tin Man and the Cowardly Lion. The RSC will use a new stage version of the story, based on the original MGM screenplay. It will include the complete film score by Harold Arlen and E. Y. Harburg, as well as material and songs written for the film but not used in the final version.

Let's all regress together and may the cash keep rolling in!

Plays of David Wood

One of the most important and prolific of writers of 'traditional' fantasy is David Wood. Among his best known works are *The Owl and the Pussycat Went to See* (1986), *Plotters of Cabbage Patch Corner* (1970), *Flibberty and the Penguin* (1971), *Hijack Over Hygenia* (1973), *The Gingerbread Man* (1976), *There Was an Old Woman* (1979), *The Meg and Mog Show* (1981) and *The Selfish Shellfish* (1983). Perhaps his most popular play is *The Gingerbread Man* which has been performed not merely by Whirligig but by a large number of repertory companies in places such as Leeds, Derby, Leicester, Chester, Dundee, Southampton, Manchester, Folkestone, Worcester and Ipswich, as well as overseas. It is a musical play with the music and lyrics also written by Wood.

The Gingerbread Man, like *Peter Pan*, involves high jinks after bedtime. It takes place on an antique dresser. The Gingerbread Man of the title has been baked by the Big Ones (the adults who own the house). He meets Salt (a sailor), Pepper (hot stuff) and Herr Von Cuckoo who lives in the cuckoo clock and is this play's principal 'problem'. He has a sore throat which is ruining his 'cuckoos', thus threatening to land him in the dreaded dustbin. The Gingerbread Man attempts to help Herr Von Cuckoo by obtaining some honey for him from the top shelf, but he meets obstruction from the Old Tea Bag, who lives a lonely, misanthropic life in a teapot. She hates the Cuckoo for waking her up at unwarranted hours. Eventually the Gingerbread Man manages to trick her. But a more formidable villain stalks the stage in the person of Sleek the Mouse (a gangster), who longs to get his teeth into succulent gingerbread. Awakened by the noise, the Big Ones conclude that there is a mouse around and drop poison on to the honey spoon. By mistake Herr Von Cuckoo eats it and the Tea Bag is called upon to help cure him with herbal remedies, at the brewing of which she is an expert. She succumbs to blandishments and thereby undergoes a conversion to social intercourse and mutual responsibility. The gang of four turn their attention to trapping and then evicting the mouse, using sweets as a bait and a propped-up mug to drop over him. The plan works. Next morning comes and the Big Ones reprieve the Cuckoo whose voice has returned and decide not to eat the Gingerbread Man. Happiness hangs heavy over the ending.

The performance of 'The Gingerbread Man' at Derby Playhouse, by the Derby Playhouse Company, 3 January 1983

The setting showed us a familiar world seen through the eyes of miniature characters, and – in proportion – the adults, being too big to show, were represented by their booming voices through loudspeakers. There was plenty of theatrical action and variety with intriguing business, dancing and whirlwind chases. There was a simple story-line to follow, and song-and-dance routines to punctuate each development. Aided and abetted by the accompanying adults, the kids made the sort of boisterous response that usually seems to mark productions of this play and is taken to indicate an enjoyable and therefore worthwhile experience. The unfolding of the action does seem to have a kind of irresistible logic. But to what end? What meanings were being created by performers and spectators?

Much is made by critics of the way Barrie seems to be using *Peter Pan* as an extension of his own personal inadequacies. *The Gingerbread Man* tells us nothing comparable about its author, and while this might be seen as healthy, the piece seems to lack the sense of the writer's having had to write it. According to Wood's own account, he was asked for the title of the new play he was to be commissioned to write. Off the cuff, he said: 'The Gingerbread Man', and then he was lumbered with it. Nor is Wood concerned to work out the political implications of the situation (as TIE/YPT plays often do) through the act of writing. There are potentially weighty themes buried in the play but they are not allowed seriously to disturb and are not addressed. The dispensers of justice with power to bind and loose were the Big Ones, whose voices boomed over the loudspeakers with a godlike authority. The Gingerbread Man was allowed to survive at the end because he had a 'cheeky' and a 'nice' face. Pity the plain ones in the audience. The Cuckoo was reprieved from redundancy by his resumption of function. It's a rough old world, though, if you're clapped out. The Tea Bag gave up her independence and was made to admit the rightness of conforming: sympathy for her was earned partly by the actress's sad face and partly by direct prompting of the audience to assure the Tea Bag that she was loved by them all. Sleek, the Mouse, was identified as a villain by his 'wide-boy' appearance. All he *did* wrong was act according to the law of his own nature. Not a play, then, that makes or even lets you stop and think. The actors at Derby unfolded thc narrative wilh such gusto and panache – as the script required – that there was not the opportunity.

When the action did stop, it was to invite the audience to participate. The kind of participation was largely peripheral. This is another example of the kind of play which, it is claimed, would not be able to continue without the co-operation of the audience. But mostly the participation in *The Gingerbread Man* was engineered so that that particular eventuality was avoided. Sometimes the adults in the audience took over the participating and ensured that the game was played according to the implicit rules. The 'autonomy' of the kids was thus compromised.

The audience was asked for suggestions as to what to use for eyes, nose and mouth in completing the Gingerbread Man at the beginning. None of them was actually taken up. Later, the audience was asked to suggest something to soothe the Cuckoo's throat, and attention was subtly drawn to the honey-pot basking in its blatantly unique appropriateness on the top shelf. Similarly, the mouse's love of sweets was the 'plant' when the audience was asked to suggest a bait to trap him. In fact the script actually says:

> Audience participation should produce the idea of food. Sleek is hungry and the scent of food would lead him anywhere. This section, led by the Gingerbread Man, will have to be improvised, depending upon the reactions and ideas of the audience. Hopefully, having established the 'food' idea, the next stage is 'what sort of food?' The audience should be guided towards the idea of something sweet – sweets!

The Mouse would, we were told, need to be 'frozen' before he could be trapped and that, for this, the audience would have help by screaming and sneezing. I personally saw a mother get first off the mark. Only once did I see a defection; it was at the end when the Cuckoo asked the audience if it would like to yodel. One (obviously sensitive) child yelled: 'No!' he was outvoted, of course. The participation was a means of checking that the audience was still awake and it was pantomimic rather than creative. We even got an 'Oh no, you're not!' when the Mouse proposed to come down. There is no reason why a play *should not* allow a young audience to determine its course but if it does not really intend to honour its promise one could argue that it would be truer to itself honestly to tell its predetermined story uninterrupted.

The Gingerbread Man, within its limits, is reasonably well written and is unpatronising. The dialogue recognises youngsters' love of word play, although on the occasion when the Mouse said: 'For days my belly's been empty and I've had a bellyful', the one solitary gaffaw came from a man. 'Through the power of the leaf see the shape of things to come' is another example (said by the soothsaying Old Tea Bag) of a line on the difficult side for the small children. The Old Tea Bag sings of Herbal Remedy:

> I can cure this malady
> With a pure herbal remedy.
> I will effect it
> With expedience
> When you've collected
> The ingredients.

So if Wood errs, it is on the side of overestimating the youngsters, and I must confess I see this as preferable to underestimating them.

There were , I felt, too many songs (ten). Sometimes, as with the Herbal Remedy song, they were integrated with the action, but sometimes they added nothing. The kids were often restless (as was I!) and one song: 'I can make you sneeze', occurring just as the trap is being set for the Mouse, rather unnecessarily slows up the momentum towards a tense climax. The music itself, though, was lively, tuneful and rhythmical.

Woods's *There Was an Old Woman* uses more of the traditional pantomime content than *The Gingerbread man*. It is described as a 'family musical' and the story as given in the published version is as follows:

> Though Mother Shipton's shoe is crowded to its laces, she lives there happily with her vast brood of children, among them Jack and Jill. Unfortunately, however, the shoe is actually the property of a Giant, who lost it and has been looking for it – with one bare foot – ever since. One day The Great Boon arrives, a genial and charming, but not terribly efficient magician, looking for a circus in which he is due to appear. His attempts to save Mother Shipton and family from the Giant involve the loss of her shoe because he is unable to bring the Giant down to normal size and harmlessness without also reducing the shoe. However, after a lot of adventures and muddled magic, all ends happily. There is even a Circus with all the acts provided by Mother Shipton's clever children.

The twists and turns of the plot are ingenious and there is continual visual and aural variety. The loudspeakers, this time, carry the Giant's booming voice and there are many songs. The story unfolds clearly and the dialogue on the whole is well judged to suit the children's powers of comprehension. There are verbal misunderstandings which appeal to both the children and the adults in the audience: Jill speaks to the reduced giant –

> JILL: Who are you?
> GIANT: Dear little lady.
> JILL: You don't look like a dear little lady to me.

Although the child audience at the performance I saw (at the Nottingham Playhouse, 25 November 1982) evinced real fear on the pet Cockerel's (Cocky's) behalf, the threatening Giant became quite lovable at the end. The audience were again invited to help on occasions, but again the participation was peripheral.

One feature of this story which was original was the presence on stage of real child actors and actresses working alongside the adult professionals. Like the Lost Boys in *Peter Pan*, Mother Shipton's protégés had lost their parents, enslaved by the Giant in this case. But, by contrast with Barrie's play, their deprivation did not reflect the personal suffering of the author and it served mainly as a step in the logic of the plot. Exposition is done by means of a communal song:

ALL: So welcome to
Our giant shoe
Where we live in peace once more
But the price it cost
Was the mums and dads we lost
When the giant waged his war.

Compare this with Barrie; Wendy has just imagined a happy return to the Darling home through the welcoming open window. Peter has felt a pain.

WENDY: Peter, what is it? [Thinking he is ill and looking lower than his chest] Where is it?

PETER: It isn't that kind of pain. Wendy you are wrong about mothers. I thought like you about the window, so I stayed away for moons and moons and then I flew back, but the window was barred for my mother had forgotten all about me and there was another little boy sleeping in my bed. [This is a general damper]

There is more for the actor to bite upon in *Peter Pan* and more ways of playing Peter's sadness in this context than are open to the children in Wood's cast. In the end, how Mother Shipton's protégés all recover their original parents is described in a stage direction.

> All suddenly stop as from offstage or over the speakers are heard footsteps running and adult cries of 'Children, Children', 'There they are'. All look off or out front to see what is happening. Then the children's faces show that they can see their parents.

The Lost Boys are, of course, adopted by Mrs Darling but Peter refuses. Mother Shipton shows regret at the loss of her 'family' but everybody is going to live in the reformed Giant's castle and happiness will reign. Wood's play evokes none of the ambivalence of attitude that Barrie's does towards the Neverland when in the final song the whole cast 'rushes on singing':

> The music starts
> The lights begin to fade
> The audience awaits the grand parade.
> Suddenly, you're in the land of make believe
> And once you're there
> You'll never want to leave.

I spoke to Chris Wallis, the director, after the show. His 'normal' job was to be in charge of the York YPT and he categorised Wood's play as 'harmless', 'conventional' and 'safe'. He did accord it an accolade on one count, however: it was entertaining. Entertainment, he said, is the 'groundrock of all children's theatre'. It was interesting to see a big name in YPT world handling a piece of children's theatre of a kind that would often have been looked upon with scorn by his fellow practioners.

Although David Wood has not, as a rule, been concerned to purvey 'messages' in his plays, *The Selfish Shellfish* goes into ecology and tackles the theme of nature conservation (compare *Arthur Rosebud's Revelation*, discussed later), particularly the threat to this from pollution. The result, according to a quotation from the *Guardian* in the publicity handout, is 'probably the most important children's play of the decade'.

The setting is a rock-pool, the denizens of which are a cantankerous old Hermit Crab ('H.C.'), his servant, Mussel, and a menacing Giant Sea Anemone. Their precarious lives are made more irksome by the arrival of human litter, and H.C.'s temper is provoked by the arrival of strangers: a Seagull, a Sea Urchin and, later, the Urchin's Aunt Starfish. He is prepared to let them stay only until the next tide and wants nothing better than to retreat again undisturbed to think out the problems of the world. The Seagull flies away only to return with the news that he has seen two tankers collide and oil spill out, a crime perpetrated by the Big Ones. He warns the inhabitants permanent and temporary, of the Rock Pool, but H.C. pays no heed. When they have settled down to sleep, Sludge, a witch-like figure, comes and Urchin, awake, is frightened and tells his Auntie. The Starfish and the Urchin are preparing to depart when the next tide brings with it the Giant Slick, of whom Sludge was the precursor. After making some menacing noises, the Slick withdraws, but promises to return again.

Next day, Mussel gets stung by the Anemone and paralysed. He needs to be treated and then moved further up the beach to be safe from the Slick, and a discarded flip-flop, once the property of a Big One, is put to use as a stretcher. Starfish has a go at H.C. for his selfish refusal to get involved even when he meets Sludge for himself. It is only when Sludge attacks him and gets trapped by the refugees in a bean-can that H.C. confesses he appreciates the favour they have done him. But the Slick is still to come, and the audience's support is craved to play upon the Slick's weakness, his vulnerability to a storm. The audience are to drum on the floor and simulate one. This they do, and the crafty Slick is whirled round and round and into the waiting jaws of the Giant Anemone. But in fighting against the Slick, the Seagull has been covered with oil and just as the others are congratulating themselves on their escape, he dies.

The performance of 'The Selfish Shellfish' at the Palace Theatre, Newark, by Whirligig Theatre Company, on the morning of 22 March 1984

Despite its shift in the direction of the concerns espoused by TIE/YPT companies, *The Selfish Shellfish* is still a play intended to be produced in a big and well-equipped theatre. Wood confesses that it was the prospect of a particular theatrical effect that really inspired him:

> I do not have a general philosophy. In many ways, my instinct is a theatrical one – in other words what 'works' theatrically. I tend to think more about that than making an obvious moral point. For instance, in *The Selfish Shellfish*, although I would agree it is a 'message' play, nevertheless what interested me in writing it was the personification of the Oil Slick and the effect on an audience of a character wearing a 30-foot square cloak which could cover the entire stage![14]

There is some experimentation with form, though. The actors get into role in full view of the audience, and the Seagull rises from the dead and stands with the others to belt out in song the final lesson. The actual song is very blatantly didactic:

> When will we learn?
> When will we learn?
> That the world
> Wasn't made
> For only you and me?
> When will we learn?
> When will it be?
> When will we learn?
> When will we see?

Wood sacrifices something of the narrative tautness of his earlier plays to develop relationships, and comment on relationships. A potentially interesting political theme is introduced as illustrated by the relationship between the Mussel and H.C.

STARFISH: I don't know how you stand it. [She looks at H.C.'s shell]

MUSSEL: H.C.? He's all right, usually. No trouble at all. But . . . well . . . the way I see it, there's thinkers and doers.

STARFISH: What do you mean?

MUSSEL: Those as think and those as do. I'm a doer. H.C.'s a thinker. We get on. We're a team.

STARFISH: But you do all the work.

MUSSEL: Exactly. He does all the thinking.

H.C. does take a hand in the necessary action later on but his conversion does not prove a deciding factor in their salvation.

However, there were only two songs and the action was effectively accompanied by piano music and this, in my opinion, considerably helped the overall pace.

Despite the Brechtian elements, Wood still treats involvment as a high priority.

> The play is very dramatic and the clash between, if you like, good and evil is a very real one, heightened by the fact that the audience have got to know and have become involved with the shellfish long before the advent of Sludge or The Great Slick. Therefore they become emotionally involved in the story and that makes the play work.[15]

The accomplished entertainer is still at work. Keith Nurse, in the *Daily Telegraph* agrees: 'That admirable children's writer, David Wood, and the Whirligig Theatre company know only too well how to keep youngsters on their toes. In doing so, they secure undivided attention and support.'[16] The entrance of Urchin from the bean-tin after exciting the curiosity of the residents of the Rock Pool and the audience is skilfully done. Sometimes Wood falls back on traditional (pantomime style) dialogue routines:

MUSSEL: Just you watch it, Urchin. He's my boss.
URCHIN: Sorry, Mussel.
MUSSEL: I'm trying to help you.
URCHIN: Sorry, Mussel.
MUSSEL: And stop saying, 'Sorry, Mussel'.
URCHIN: Sorry, Mussel. Whoops.

There are tired old participation routines, too. The audience is requested to help trap Sludge in the bean-tin. (Remember Sleek, the Mouse?) At Newark, the children in the audience perversely tried to warn Sludge by yelling: 'It's a trap!' Some of those at Derby Playhouse did a similar service for the Tea Bag when the hero, the Gingerbread Man, was stealing her honey. A heartening sign of 'autonomy'?

The big question is whether Wood has sufficiently modified his characteristic forms to suit his new theatrical aim. The setting was 'beautiful', of the kind that is Wood's hallmark. In this context, even the litter – the bean-can and the flip-flop – underwent a sea change, and when the flip-flop was formally identified for them the children obviously thought it was cute. Familiar, too, was the adoption of the point of view of the smaller creatures of the world. The Big Ones had now become the baddies, but they did not appear in body or voice. I found the play somewhat confusing in its effect. The Slick was terrifying and had at least one child being hurried out by a teacher. When the audience were asked to help banish the Slick by pretending to be a storm, it was basically the same old con trick only this time it was not scheduled to produce results. The Slick was defeated by nature, and his demise made a joke of, as he was swallowed, with a burp, by the Giant Sea Anemone. This is at odds with the exhortations of the song which imply that we can do something about pollution. One is reminded of the hortatory address to the audience in *Susumu's Story* which also urges an audience with no political clout to take action, but the kind of play it is makes the message more inevitable. The connection of the evil Slick with the now remote Big Ones is a difficult one to make. The litter on the beach did look beautifully transformed and it served useful purposes in the end, the bean-can to trap the Sludge and the flip-flop to serve as a stretcher for the stung Mussel. The death of the Seagull is a bold stroke on Wood's part. I am not sure whether the logic of the play can easily take it, though. It jarred a bit in Newark and visibly upset some of the audience in an unconstructive way. There is nothing potentially antipathetic to seriousness in the animal fable as such, but the dangers of tweeness and sentimentality are ever present.

> Music as Seagull enters at the top of the rock. He wears a black cloak of 'oil'. He stumbles painfully to the centre of the pool. The others watch in stunned silence. Seagull collapses. He has a couple of convulsions, and is then still . . . Starfish rushes to him. She listens to his chest and shakes her head. He is dead. The shellfish move sadly to each other humming the 'when will we learn tune'. They all hold hands in grief.

Pantomime

It is when we look at the pantomime, with which Wood's work invites comparison, that we appreciate that his achievement has real quality. He often makes use of the some sort of material – well-known fairy-tales and nursery rhymes – goes for theatrical spectacle as the pantomime does, lards his plays with songs and contrives a happy ending. He also dedicates his shows to a 'family' audience and, as do pantomimes, he usually plays to a full house.

But the pantomime interrupts its story to allow for set comic or 'magic' pieces and 'personalities' doing their thing. The open participation it invites is all part of a game. It has its female principal boy – for which Barrie had no cause to be thankful. Its goodies are impossibly lovable; it prefers its villains to be recognisable so as to shift all responsibility for evil on to them. The tone is usually a mixture of jokiness and sentimentality. The panto and Wood have the same problem of how to appeal both to children and adults. Too often the panto addresses the adults (often with suggestive humour) over the kids' heads. The adults in Wood's audiences are usually pretty vocal, but towards the children Wood behaves with commendable integrity. Although he needs the money, he is choosy about the means he employs to get it.

It is usually assumed that it is inappropriate to apply the artistic standards that one would apply to a (musical) play to the panto, and critics often judge a pantomime a success if it seemed to send customers away satisfied and sold a lot of seats. But of late, critics have started to require more in the way of aesthetic quality. Pantos are praised when they achieve a multi-level effect and are condemned for a split-level approach. Carol Wilks, writing about *The Land of Oz* at Leeds Playhouse, says:

> The Playhouse production spin-off of *The Wizard Oz* cheeringly sets itself in a dreamland where comical and magical things happen, designed to appeal to kids first and adults later. This, in Rex Doyle's production is a simple recipe for pantomime success which other companies might do well to follow.

She found 'the jokes are child-sized and work the better for it'.[17] Joyce McMillan writes:

Big commercial pantos inhabit an uneasy no-man's land these days. On the one hand there's the conviction that panto ought to be an entertainment for children with all the necessary innocence, magic and simple narrative that entails; on the other hand, there's the economic necessity of attracting adult audiences through a long winter season.[18]

And Cordelia Oliver:

To keep both juveniles and their parents happy is a perennial problem with pantomimes. The kids get easily bored when the story line is broken for songs and what they see as slushy love-interest and often enough the comedian's jokes are strictly for adults.[19]

Joyce McMillan also requires a strong story line. Writing of *The Ugly Duckling* at Irvine she says:

I daresay there are explanations for the miserable, half-baked state of this script, not least the fact that this is 'just a kids' show' and a harmless Christmas frolic. But as the irritable, three-jumps-ahead response of the audience at the Magnum Centre demonstrated, children are if anything more demanding than an adult audience, less polite, less tolerant, and more vulnerable to the disappointments of a poorly told story.[20]

And of *Peter and Penny's Panto* performed at the same theatre, also by Borderline Company, she writes:

The plot – which concerns the theft of the magician's wand by a villain called the Great Bahooky and its recovery by Peter and Penny, a pair of clockwork dolls, magically brought to life – is as thin as paper, lacking both the traditional richness of the big pantomime stories and their mythical, fairytale resonance.[21]

Sometimes a writer will change the original well-known plot but not always for artistic ends or with pleasing artistic results. Reviewing *Jack and the Beanstalk* for the Arts Council in the version I saw at the Crucible Theatre, Sheffield, on 22 December 1986, I said:

> The storyline almost disappears in this family pantomime, but what there is of it alters the traditional story in ways that weaken it. Jack is cheated by the villain, Fleshcreep, into believing that he has received a bag of gold for the cow and this gold is later turned into beans. This lost the psychological interest of Jack's being to blame. Later, Fleshcreep turns out not to represent the giant but – in Wizard of Oz style – to *be* the giant, or rather his voice. He also becomes a goodie in the end. A safe, pleasant but unexciting version. No tremor of real fear, no 'danger'.

Joyce McMillan praises Rikki Fulton's version of *Cinderella* at Edinburgh King's Head for giving the story an uncharacteristic dramatic weight.

> His main device is to provide the story with a real villainess in the shape of Cinderella's wicked stepmother, thus freeing the Uglies from their uncomfortable obligation to provide a focus for the panto's evil forces as well as for its comedy. This opens the way to some pretty relaxed and self-indulgent comic interludes as well as to a more dramatic treatment of the main plot.[22]

This critic fearlessly applies the criterion of imaginative truth to a genre customarily thought exempt from it.

> Meanwhile, down at the 'serious' end of the business the big unspoken question hovering over this year's panto season is whether all this love, magic, and changes of heart has any meaning for the kids of central Scotland today. Or whether the only kind of change that is likely to do them any good grows out of the barrel of a gun.
>
> The Citizen's theatre's version of *Red Riding Hood* – written by Myles Rudge and directed with great vigour and integrity by Giles Havergal – tackles the issue head-on with a firm assertion that power without love is a meaningless prize and that by adopting the oppressor's methods of cruelty, vengeance and ruthlessness we lose touch with the very values we're fighting for.
>
> In this clever version of the story, the little heroine, Anna, and her brother, Peter, children of a poor clock-maker, wander into a frightening dream-world where the ruthless local landowner takes on the shape of a vicious wolf-man. Anna's magic Red Riding Hood – magic only because it's been stitched with love by her dear old granny – protects her from the wolf, but Peter, a discontented little exponent of the politics of envy, is seduced away from his family by the wolf's offers of earthly power and influence. He heads off for the castle where he sprouts a new hairy ear or tail with every cruel deed he does. Brave Anna follows, determined to win him back.
>
> Havergal is too wise a director to scorn the great strengths of the panto tradition – the battle of good and evil, the slapstick, the music, the audience participa-

> tion. But he also succeds spectacularly in injecting some real modern siginficance into the format – on the opening night the show gradually won the kids from open doubt and cynicism about the value of Anna's mission to her final struggle for Peter's soul. That kind of risk-taking in performance is the hallmark of really brave and classy children's theatre.[23]

Ms McMillan puts 'the unspoken questions' herself. As she says, the mere fact of taking on the *Red Riding Hood* story is an act of courage on the company's part. The story has deep sexual resonances and a disturbing anti-male bias which must be come to terms with. Red Riding Hood's journey is a journey into sexual experience and it was sufficiently 'adult' in its concerns to inspire Angela Carter's film script *Company of Wolves*.

The Citizens Theatre production of *Red Riding Hood* may have preserved familiar conventions as a foundation for a new and different construct but it was still an 'occasion' in a main house setting. For an even more radical departure one has to look at the work of some community and YPT groups. In 1983, Mansfield-based Perspectives toured local community centres with *Niddala*, which, if you reverse the letters, proves to be a new, devised version of *Aladdin*. I caught up with them at Eckington Community Centre.

The set could not afford to be spectacular. It was a cut-out elephant but it was put to varied use. The Queen in the story took one of her daughters (Niddala) to live – anonymously – the lives of commoners. The other daughter was left to rule. The Evil One attempted to get his hands on their valuable possession, the magic lamp, ended up in mortal combat with the Queen and fell with her into a lake of fire. The group made an attempt at cracking the problem of the multi-level appeal. There were satirical shafts for the adults to enjoy and the Queen's propensity for slumming it provided a fairly obvious vehicle for a political message. For the children, there was what slapstick a small stage permits. However, the performance did not knit satisfactorily and it lurched uneasily between the near-tragic and traditional pantomime flippancy. May Rao, as the Queen, and Alan Turton, as the Evil One, seemed to belong to different plays. The cast, though, played with versatility and commitment, and the transformations were the product of the actors' skills and not of some ingenious machinery. In that sense, what we were seeing was another kind of theatrical 'magic', the magic of the theatrical process itself, surely the most awe-inspiring magic in the end. Forty adults and twenty children saw the performance the night I attended, a small enough audience to challenge the actors' power to form an intimate rapport.

Another play which tried to give a new meaning to an old fairy-story was *Changing Gear*, written by Ruth Craft for the Merseyside YPT. Like the pantomime, it was laced with music, song and dance, but it was aimed at a specific (young) age group (11–13) and was taken into schools. In the publicity handout, the new version of the Cinderella story was given as follows:

> Three sisters lived alone because their mother has died and their father stays out. Fizz and Baby Blue spend all their money on clothes and other luxuries. Zippa tries to help but they think he's wet. Cinderella, who is mad about aeroplanes, hates working at the pet-shop. She lectures her sisters from up the ladder where she goes to get away from them.

Kevin is opening Prince Charming's Wine Bar for cool people who don't get too close, and he's looking for girls to work there. Fizz and Baby Blue want to be invited and Fizz invents a new dance called the Frazz to impress him.

On Saturday night, they spend hours at the mirror putting on make-up and rush off to the Wine Bar. Zippa tells Cinderella that she should try to understand her sisters' feelings and see if they could get on better. He admits that he's too soft and does things for other people so that they will like him. They both decide to risk changing things. The local Wish Administrator explains the difference between magic wishes and wishes which might come true if you try. She gives Zippa and Cinderella a chance try out their wishes: she flies the Concorde and he grows a tomato.

The opening night at the Wine Bar is a failure. Although Prince Charming doesn't have any real customers he tries to make Fizz and Baby Blue join in with his pretence. He gets Fizz to fetch some stolen sandals to sell. Everything goes wrong and Fizz and Baby Blue realise how stupid they were to have been taken in, and go home.

Cinderella and Zippa have waited up for them and the three sisters try to be nicer to each other. Prince Charming tries to con them into hiding the stolen sandals but they refuse.

The 'meaning' of the play was explained thus:

'Dressing up and putting it on' – the outside trappings of clothes, music, dance and style – are often a cloak to hide the people we really are. Our next play for 11–13 year-olds looks from outside in to examine why and how both girls and boys are subtly pressured into roles they may not always wish to play.

The performance of 'Changing Gear' at St Ambrose Barlow High School, Liverpool, by the Merseyside Young People's Theatre, 8 February, 1983

The audience consisted of boys from one school mixed with girls from another. The setting was almost in the round and the seating well raked. There was a sideboard and a stepladder.

To open, the company socked the audience with a chauvinistic song:

Birds, birds, birds, birds
Use a lot of complicated words,
Say a lot of things better left unsaid,
Let their stupid feelings rule their head.

As an example of such feminine behaviour, we were introduced to the sisters Fizz, in a ra-ra skirt and red hair, and Baby Blue, carrying a cuddly toy, expressing worries about their appearance and singing a self-reassuring song: 'My face is ace'. Zippa, a young lad, turned up, and next Cinderella herself, wearing a striped blazer. She talked of her dead mother and was reprimanded by Fizz for indulging in 'messy feelings' and striking attitudes. The dialogue was self-consciously earthy and was based on the local patois. Cinderella was referred to by Fizz as a 'smarmy little git' (not exactly 'complicated words'). In fact *all* the sisters sneered unpleasantly at each other, presumably to give them something to progress to later. Cinderella went up the ladder and threw paper aeroplanes around (significant image?)

Kevin entered with his offer of work at the Prince Charming Wine Bar. Fizz demonstrated her new dance and the audience laughed.

Zippa (Mr Nice Guy) told Cinderella that she was something of a bully to her sisters. Cinderella accused Kevin of crime, stealing things and using the profits for his club. She complained of being 'left out' of things, but if this was supposed to win the audience's sympathy, it failed. It was difficult to care about this character; she was too spoilt. I noticed spreading inattention among the youngsters and quelling looks from the teachers.

One factor which made it difficult to sympathise with anybody was the compulsive and abrasive comedy. Cinderella hated working in the pet-shop and talked of hamsters as having 'gobs stuffed full of muck'. That is partly why Cinderella's would-be soulful song was out of key.

Zippa urged Cinderella to try to understand her sisters. Cinderella went on to the attack with, 'You look stupid, letting people walk all over you'. She sneered at him for 'creeping'. He was afraid of doing things in case he should be put down. Zippa comes back angrily with the accusation that Cinderella did not care about other people's feelings. Zippa's anger was unprepared for, dramatically speaking, and the moralising was becoming very explicit. As a result of the forensic interchange, Cinderella was less sure she was right and decided to risk taking the ladder down and getting to know her sisters and herself better. Perhaps Zippa would risk asking his girlfriend for a date and telling his parents he wanted to stay on and do A levels at school. Cinderella's ambition was to be an airline pilot and Zippa wanted to be a horticulturist. The ladder was getting to seem a very obviously set-up symbol.

There was a considerable stir, though, when the Fairy Godmother arrived and flashed a silver suit. She introduced herself as the Wish Fulfiller for the District, delivered a homily on wishing and claimed to handle best the kind of wish that *can* come true rather than the day-dream wish-fulfilment. Despite intentions and disclaimers, there was an aura of magic about her, and a Disney-like way of talking was out of key with expectations raised so far. Cinderella, on her ladder, acted out flying Concorde and Zippa acted out growing an entire garden in one night. The intruder left the stage.

In the Wine Bar, Kevin talked to two plywood cut-out customers about Spanish holidays and got the girls to do their dance for them. A stagey device, which did not quite work. Kevin then sent Fizz to fetch the stolen sandals to sell around the Diamond Disco. The girls, though, had had enough and they turned on him. A significant development!

At home the girls and Zippa became all matey. Not that the actresses pointed this or rendered any surprise. They just accepted it. As happy an ending as one could hope for from a pantomime, but it came about by way of several feats of plot-engineering.

I found this a somewhat incoherent, inconsistent and contrived performance. Paul Harman, the director of this and the Merseyside YPT, thought the play had too many themes at first and had to be simplified. It was supposed to be 'about' the sort of roles people would like or were able to take (for example the airline pilot and the horticulturist). Harman himself wants his play to show the possibility of individuals changing. He thinks 'images' can help to bring this about. I found the moralising message too stark, the tone of the play uncertain, the developments willed rather than evolved, the symbolism too insistent and the elements of the Cinderella story (for example Fairy Godmother and slipper) clumsily dragged in.

The audience was invited to make comments at the end of the performance. The boys would have preferred more action (more matter with less polemic, song and dance and so on). The girls thought it a bit young for them.

To be generous, what we did have was a brave attempt to be relevant and original, an attempt to make the set functional rather than a mere spectacle and to include the language really used by men (and women).

Fairy-tales and nursery rhymes, then, have been used as a loose framework to contain a variety of comic or sentimental set-pieces and as vehicles for a challenging view of human relationships. A play may have a modern setting and rely on the audience's knowledge of the original story so that they will appreciate the meaning of the changes. Shaw, in *Pygmalion* uses the Cinderella story in a way that disturbs the expectations and frustrates the desire for a romantic happy ending by not, after all, marrying off Eliza Doolittle and Professor Higgins.

A related branch of traditional fantasy treated in theatre for the young, that of myth and legend, seems to have invited less in the way of emotional distortion and trivialisation. One thinks of the sterling work of Allan Cullen in the 1960s with the Greek myths or of John Wiles with *The Golden Masque of Agamemnon*. The myths and legends embody some enduring truths about human nature and human society and can hold particular fascination for children at certain ages. As John Holt says:

Ten is a heroic age for most kids. They remind me in many ways of the Homeric Greeks. They are quarrelsome and combative; they have a strong and touchy sense of honour; they believe that every affront must be paid with interest; they are fiercely loyal to their friends, even though they may change friends often; they have little sense of fair play, and greatly admire cunning and trickery; they are both highly possessive and very generous – no smallest trifle may be taken from them but they are likely to give anything away, if they feel so disposed. Most of the time, they don't feel like little children and they don't like being talked to as if they were little children.[24]

Hiawatha

One of the best-known adaptations of a legend for the stage and one addressed to a child audience in the first place was Michael Bogdanov's version of the Hiawatha story. Based on Longfellow's poem *Hiawatha,* the play was first performed by the Young Vic Company on 20 November 1978 and later transferred to the National Theatre (the Olivier auditorium) on 10 December 1980. It has been revived as a seasonal (Christmas) offering on subsequent occasions and was the first children's play to be taken by the company on tour.

The story concerns the Iroquois hero, Hiawatha, famous for his deeds of honour and daring and for uniting the Indian tribes. Gitche Manito, the Indian god, calls on the Indians to make peace with each other and proposes to send a Prophet. An Indian woman, Nokomis, gives birth to a daughter, Wenonah, who is wooed by Mudjekeewis, the West Wind, is deserted by him and dies in sorrow. Nokomis brings up the child of the union, Hiawatha, and Iagoo, the boaster, makes him a bow with which he kills his first roebuck, a feat for which he is feted. Curious about his father, he is informed by his grandmother that Mudjekeewis became the West Wind after he had defeated the Great Bear, keeper of the Belt of Wampum. Hiawatha says he will go to his father and avenge the slight to his mother. He engages in combat with Mudjekeewis, but the West Wind cannot be killed. So impressed, though, is his father that he promises Hiawatha a share in his kingdom 'as Death draws near'. Homeward bound, Hiawatha meets the maiden, Minehaha, a momentous and memorable event in his life. We meet Hiawatha's friends, the singer, Chibiabos, and the strong man, Kwasind. Hiawatha builds a canoe and sets off to kill the sturgeon, Nahma, only to be swallowed by it along with his craft. With his fist he destroys the fish's heart and is rescued from his prison by seagulls who prize open the jaws. Hiawatha now returns to seek out Minhaha, asks her father for her hand and marries her and takes her home. At home, we meet Pau-Puk-Keewis, the 'merry mischief-maker' who beats Iagoo, the boaster, at gaming and wins his nephew as an attendant. Pau-Puk-Keewis embarks on a mischief-making spree in which he kills Hiawatha's guardian raven while Hiawatha is absent and thus insults him in a manner which his honour cannot brook. Hiawatha sets off after Pau-Puk-Keewis and thinks that he has killed the Beaver that Pau-Puk-Keewis has changed himself into, but the wily fellow has moved to a different body, that of a swan. Unfortunately, the swan flies in an element where Hiawatha has influence and soon he is dashed, dead, to the ground. Famine next strikes the Indian tribe and Minehaha dies and is buried. At the end of the play, Iagoo, the boaster, talks of the approaching white man whom he has seen on his travels, and his tales are confirmed by Hiawatha who has seen him in a vision. The time comes for Hiawatha to be transported, in his canoe, to the Isles of the Blessed.

The performance of 'Hiawatha' at the National Theatre, by the National Theatre Company, 23 December 1982

I found myself as a member of a not over-full morning audience of a variety of ages, tending towards the younger end, and a variety of nationalities, particularly visiting Americans. There was a fair sprinkling of adults. Although it is dangerous to make sweeping generalisations about the social 'class' of the clientele, it cost me £4.50 for a ticket, expensive at that time.

The performance had much to offer at all levels, judging by the rapt attention of the children and my own reactions as an adult. Jack Cross in the *Guardian* makes the same point:

> Older readers will not fail to catch echoes of Arthur, Cuchulain (and perhaps, Christ) in the legendary Hiawatha, hero of a world in the throes of heartless change. Children will miss much of the symbolism . . . and respond more immediately to the high drama and the delicately inserted passages of low humour.[25]

In fact, *Hiawatha* had something of the appeal of pantomime. The huge auditorium was awe-inspiring but the children were jumping on and off the stage in the interval, so the ground was not completely holy.

The script is published (by Heinemann) but Bogdanov aims to make his statement in terms of total theatre, the sort of prestige spectacular that the National Theatre is equipped to mount. The visual and aural effects were, for the most part, entrancing and exhilarating. The stage was an open stage, large in area, and the basic setting was that of a huge Indian tepee, which defined the main acting area, with a monster sun-disc behind. Lighting subtly changed the moods, atmosphere and season, and images stamped themselves on the mind. The West Wind, standing high before the disc with waving sheets of white silk before him and pictures of clouds swirling past behind him, while a howling fills the auditorium, is an example. Minehaha's death was quite haunting. Snowflakes of light came slowly down, settling in a white sheet on the ground, while a blue light touched the poles of the tepee and suggested the bare trunks of the forest trees and stuck a chill of fear into the audience. A sequence of undulating poles vividly created the river through which Hiawatha chased the beaver. The Indians entered the acting area at the beginning of each act stomping in a line to the accompaniment of a crescendo of drums, a stunning way to capture the audience's attention. Drums, too, accompanied the speaking of the narrative, reinforcing its rhythmical qualities. I felt, though, that there was some fascination on the director's part with visuals for their own sake. When Gitche, the god, told the tribes to wash the bloodstains from their faces, I did not feel we needed reminding what colour water and blood were with blue and red silken streamers, for instance. The children got restless during Chibiabos's song, the words of which were incomprehensible anyway. Generally, the visual and aural effects were in harmony with the words, and the one was paced to suit the other. It has been customary for re viewers to praise Bogdanov for bestowing creative life on a dead nineteenth-century narrative poem, but, although he has added some lines of his own, he is well served by his source material. It is the words that dignify the fate of

Pau-Puk-Keewis, withdrawing us from the emotionally ambivalent triumph of Hiawatha and according the mischief-maker the status of legend.

> And the name of Pau-Puk-Keewis
> Lingers still among the people,
> Lingers still among the singers
> And among the story-tellers;
> And in Winter, when the snowflakes
> Whirl in eddies round the lodges,
> When the wind, in gusty tumult
> O'er the smoke-flues pipes and whistles
> 'There', they cry, 'comes Pau-Puk-Keewis
> He is dancing through the village –
> He is gathering in his harvest!'

Without the words, it would not be at all clear what was happening to Hiawatha at the end, that he is, in fact, dying. The words both explain and interpret the event.

The 'meaning' that the children might take away is a summation of the signals that the performance gives out. They were invited to admire and approve of Hiawatha'a heroism, his prowess and his sense of duty, although it was not always understood why he felt to strongly about some things and acted as he did. The themes include the archetypal opposition of son to father, but the wooing, desertion and death of Wenonah was done in such a brief visual ritual (she turned away and was shrouded in a black cloak) that it was hard to appreciate the offence that Hiawatha had suffered. The reality of death as a harsh fact of existence came home uncompromisingly when it happened to Minehaha and the incident was given some weight. When Mudjekeewis killed the bear, though, the pantomime style of the episode, with loud bops as club hit head, was designed to lessen the impact on the audience. The trouble was that we were asked to believe it had really died and yet also to accept that it could rise like Tom the cat (in *Tom and Jerry* cartoons) as good as new and do a dance. At least the children's laughter was friendly and not derisory. The message of the desirability of peace and brotherhood came powerfully over, as did that of harmony with nature. Throughout the performance there was a joyous celebration of the life of the body. Various bullies, such as Nahma, the sturgeon, got their comeuppance, but it seemed hard that Pau-Puk-Keewis, who was allowed to establish himself as a likeable rogue, had to die for his pranks.

Despite the pantomime elements, there were few direct appeals to the audience for support or sympathy, and this was a wise decision as the action made its own powerful impact. As an unconscious tribute to the empathy achieved, children in the interval were stomping, Indian-like on their way to their fruit juice. Parents and chaperones in the audience had their uses. When Hiawatha was inside the sturgeon, I heard one child ask his dad who put the hero in prison. Obviously neither word nor image had been clear to this child. Of more questionable value was the parent who explained to his child that what he saw were not really snowflakes but strobe lights. One is reminded of Lawrence's advice about the sort of answer to give a child who asks why grass is green. You do not go on about chlorophyl, but tell him 'because it is'.

The young audience, when I was there, was very attentive on the whole. Jack Cross thought the same of the audience at a subsequent performance at the Birmingham Hippodrome:

As every actor knows, an audience made up of school parties is not an easy ride. And as every teacher knows, conducting such groups is rarely a soft option. But there were no doubts on either side of the foot lights last Tuesday, when the National Theatre began its first ever tour for children with *Hiawatha*. A crop-haired ten-year-old, who had been wriggling about distributing the last of his smarties as the lights came up, delivered his first and last opinion on the production. 'It was magic', he said.[26]

I saw the performance again when its tour reached Sheffield. Because of the boldly thrusting Crucible stage, some of the audience were looking not deep into a mysterious and exotic world, but at the spectators opposite. It was an expensive evening 'do' (a middle-class event) and half the audience were adults. The effect was more intimate and by now the actors were putting in more comic touches, but the kids enjoyed them without disorderly behaviour.

However, as has been said, a play means what performers and spectators between them make it mean. Some theatregoers had different experiences. In a letter to the *Guardian* Hazel Wilkinson wrote:

> I have seen the play three times, twice with children in holiday times, once with another adult and a capacity audience of children . . . If I hadn't been to *Hiawatha* when the school parties were there I would have agreed with every word of the article, and I still think *Hiawatha* is a wonderful production that works on many levels and has much to offer both to children (who are willing to listen) and to adults.
>
> However, the schoolchildren I encountered did not listen well – many seemed to think they were watching

television and it wouldn't matter if they commented out loud. When there was any drumming, they began to clap with the drums. This would not have mattered if they had also stopped with the drums, but the end of the drumming invariably became the cue for general clapping and whistling, thus the next dialogue was lost in the hubbub.

I felt that the actors found this difficult to cope with, since the play is rather like a ritual and must continue to keep up the rhythm; it is unlike a pantomime or many plays where it is possible for the actor to address the audience directly and to some extent orchestrate their responses.[27]

Pat Friday, who was doing research, at the University of Warwick, into school parties in theatres, also felt moved to make a contribution:

I have read with growing interest the debate about *Hiawatha*. I have seen it twice, once in London and once in Birmingham and on both occasions the audience was composed of school parties, but the experiences were worlds apart. At one performance, the atmosphere was truly 'magic'; at the other (Birmingham on Thursday, incidentally) the magic had been replaced by interesting 'theatrical effects'.

Hiawatha is visually stunning and is a skilful, varied and imaginative portrayal of the poem. So what was wrong? Not even this production can complete with numerous groups of children who, from the beginning, talked at normal volume on wide-ranging topics.

The Great Bear did gain their attention momentarily but any more sinister moment became virtually inaudible as the level of noise in the auditorium seemed to

> rise in inverse proportion to the level of lighting on the stage. One six-year-old solved the problem by going to sleep until his teacher hit him on the head with a programme.
>
> I should like to open up the debate into the whole problem of why schools' audiences behave the way they sometimes do. Does the fault lie with the pupils, the theatres or the teachers? Many pupils seem unaware of the demands made on them by the theatrical medium; theatres ensure that the interval is a time to replenish stocks of crisps, sweets and canned drinks; some teachers do not make sufficient effort to control parties – though this is made impossible when theatres give bookings which stretch from one side of the auditorium to the other.[28]

There does seem to be an art in being an audience! When adults are present, there is a fine line for them to tread between disciplining the youngsters and steering their responses and letting them react spontaneously according to how they perceive the significance of what is going on.

5
New Fantasy

Plays in this category adopt the fantasy mode but invent new material. Often, the fantastic events take place in a known and recognisable world. Fantasy of this kind can be used to explore contemporary or timeless issues or themes very directly. (In some respects, David Wood's *The Selfish Shellfish* qualifies to be in this chapter also.) The writer of newly invented fantasy may experience a freedom .to create new meanings denied to somebody cramped by the rules of naturalism. But if he has a message to deliver, he may be tempted to take short cuts and juggle with the material in too deliberate and arbitrary a manner.

Common Stock has the reputation of consistently mounting 'plays for children of the sort of idiosyncratic, challenging and unpatronising kind that writers on the fringe are well placed to produce but which most of the media is disposed to ignore'. It 'bases most of its work on improvisations, discussions and workshops with local children and, from its London home, tours the country'.[1]

2. *Old King Cole* by Ken Campbell (photograph © Jerry Wellington).

The Goldfish Bowl, one of their efforts, came about by this means. It was intended for seven- to fourteen-year-olds – a fair spread! The workshops had been on subjects such as pollution, food and so on, and the story had been pulled together by writer, Kate Vandergrift, and director, John Blatchely. A team of three actresses and two actors (one coloured) performed.

The performance of 'The Goldfish Bowl' at Sudbury Hall in Derbyshire, by Common Stock Theatre Company, 28 July 1982

The performance actually took place in the open air with the Hall as backdrop. It was a fine, sunny afternoon. No beguiling darkness, no fancy lighting. Mainly the actors and their bodies. A simple, versatile set to represent outside and inside a goldfish bowl and later a café.

Mother encouraged her small daughter (Cordelia) to save money and Cordelia decided to drop her savings into the goldfish bowl for safety. 'Why did Daddy go away?' she asked her mother. Mother replied: 'He was a little confused.' The adults in the audience laughed. The kids did not seem to get the joke.

Water-bubbling noises heralded the entry of the fish in their bowl. Clever use of trembling hands. Without the massive back-up of David Wood scenery, the actors were thrown on their own resources. The fish were Sid and Solly, Solly being Jewish and played by the coloured actor, according to the logic of the day. Cordelia's coins landed in the fishes' bowl – a neat bit of linkage. A declaration by them to the effect that 'we represent the entire population of this poor polluted bowl' explicitly brought in one of the themes in somewhat high-pitched language. (The later statement that 'the more awful the conditions, the closer we get to real democracy' is even more difficult for the younger end of the audience.) The population was augmented by the arrival of Lola, from a plastic bag, who regained the flagging attention with some eye-catching movement.

There was now a big, unheralded and rather confusing time-jump. Cordelia had grown up and was in a black dress, ready to go to the opera. A Mr Francobelli had joined the cast, a fat foreigner (played by the coloured actor) interested in Cordelia's mother. He warned Cordelia about her diet: 'If you eat sweets, you get fat lika da fat weemen.' The blatant irony of such a pronouncement from the like of him escaped the kids. Irony can be difficult for the very young. Francobelli gave Cordelia a bangle which she deposited in the goldfish bowl. He was not satisfied with the security of the arrangment and he proposed to introduce some piranha fish. In the bowl, Lola was teaching the fish to dance when a piranha arrived and ate Sid. The audience received the event in a matter-of-fact way; Lola 'cried' but without much emotion, and she straightway got down to teaching Solly to fight. Solly fought and the piranha retired defeated.

Next, the scene moved to a café and introduced a new character, Dog. He was an emaciated animal and made a stark contrast with the overblown Cordelia eating her ice-cream. He opined that 'fat is beautiful'. Cordelia, though, said that when you get fat nobody loves you. She was hoarding money against her old age, since, when she was old, nobody would love her then either (especially if she was fat as well). To add to Cordelia's insecurity Mum and Francobelli had gone off and left her. (Why?)

It turned out that Dog was working for a circus, collecting new acts. If he did not come up with the goods, he was threatened with ejection on his 'moth-eaten ears'.

But the fish (remember them?) showed their dance and Cordelia was signed up as the Fat Lady. She was still not loved for herself, though. Dog did not take her on out of affection but with an eye to the business opportunity. The sturdy moral was something along the lines of the desirability of settling for what you are, and 'Not too little, not too much.' The fish did not die of pollution and Sid only indirectly as a consequence of Cordelia's 'greed' (or was it thrift?). A fairly grim picture of the world for youngsters. One does not want false reassurance even for children, but is the loveless picture in fact convincing?

Rosalind Asquith, writing of Common Stock's products, says: 'The complexity of structure and imagination may be the reverse, theatrically, of the fine detailing and psychological analysis of naturalism but it is by no means inferior.'[2] Nevertheless, it might have been interesting to know why Dad had deserted the family and why Mum and Francobelli had deserted Cordelia. Complexity of structure and choice of setting may sacrifice clarity and accessibility. Concern for theme and issue, for what is going to be learned by the audience, may override the narrative to such a degree that the children have nothing to hang on to.

In the plays we have looked at in detail, there has been some attempt to incorporate death or the threat of death into the picture of human experience. Peter Pan recorded his subjective expectations. Hiawatha went through death to immortality, but Minehaha and several others ceased to exist except, in the case of Pau-Puk-Keewis, as legends. The seagull in *The Selfish Shellfish* was victim whose death was meant to convert from grief to anger and to inspire preventive action on the part of the audience. Sid, the goldfish in *The Goldfish Bowl*, was partly a victim of bad luck, lack of correct training and materialism. Death of ourselves and others is a fact that most people find difficulty in accommodating to and accepting. But even young children may be faced with its immediate prospect and may be forced in the end to decide into what perspective it throws all the rest of their experience.

There is a growing awareness in educational circles of the need in the classroom for some confrontation with this difficult area.

> School timetables today include lectures and discussions on abortion, abnormal sex practices, drug and alcohol abuse – all of which can and do lead to death. Yet death as a classroom topic has been largely ignored or rejected. Now the subject is an implicit part of the new GCSE syllabuses which, though varying across the five school boards, all include sections on Divorce, Suicide, Euthanasia and worldwide religious customs. To help teachers handle this 'last taboo' with understanding and openness, Barbara Ward and Jamie Houghton, in association with Cruse, have published *Good Grief – Talking and Learning about Loss and Death*. The authors – Barbara Ward, senior health officer for more than 100 schools, and Jamie Houghton, chaplain and head of religious studies at a comprehensive school – say that loss and death education has become an important part of the school curriculum in the United States. But 'there is no recognised scheme for teaching the subject in this country'. The need, they believe, is urgent now that one in five children faces divorce of parents; 200,000 children under 16 have lost a parent through death; 750 per 100,000 in the 15–19 age group try suicide (more than twice as many as 10 years ago) and youngsters are also faced with losses,

> such as no job. In addition, they are daily confronted by death in the media. They are not taught how to react.[3]

A good play – even for children – will present a view of the world in which death at least *could* occur. By way of reassurance, such a play would also affirm the value and importance of life. There have been earnest and worthy attempts on the part of children's playwrights and theatre companies to take death not just as a necessary part of the package deal but as the subject of the play. Such impinging material may depend for its success on the dramatist's own ability (and the actors') to cope with the notion. The writer of the article in the *Guardian* just quoted believes that their classroom colleagues may have the same problem:

> The authors [of *Good Grief*] suggest that maybe teachers can't cope with their own fears and attitudes in breaching the taboo, reserving the topic of death mainly for religious studies. They note that, 'in one of our pilot schemes a 15-year-old girl cried in class. Her father had died two years before and this was the first time anyone in the school had mentioned it.'[4]

If, as they hope, the writer and the stage artists are to exorcise their audience's fear and ignorance they will have to strike the right note and play with real conviction. *Dead Easy* by Ursula Jones and *The Arkansaw Bear*, by the American playwright Aurand Harris, both choose the form of 'invented fantasy' which makes possible a directness of thematic treatment. Both present death as a personification, a device hallowed in 'adult' drama from *Everyman* to *The Seventh Seal*.

The performance of 'Dead Easy' at Tinsley Primary School, Sheffield, by the Sheffield Crucible Vanguard Company, 18 November 1982

When they came into the light, airy hall and sat on the horseshoe of chairs and benches, the audience of eight to nine year olds, and some teachers, were greeted with an eye-catching set in the shape of a brightly coloured fairground scene, with a shining gold roundabout and a tent and dodgem cars. At the side was a table with a tape-recorder on it where the sound technician could operate in full view. The total cast consisted of one man and four women, the man playing a multiplicity of roles and narrating. The story, we were told, was to be Karen's. Karen was played by a coloured actress, a fact which could earn a bonus on this occasion, with an audience of this particular composition, as half the children were Pakistanis.

Karen and a friend enjoyed themselves at the fair. By throwing balls into a gaping mouth, Karen won a goldfish in a plastic bag. We gathered that while Karen was so wrapped up in her own enjoyment, her gran was to be taken into hospital where there was every possibility she would die.

We moved to Karen's home where mother was packing Gran's things, and a very explicit discussion about death took place with Karen asking probing questions like: 'Have you ever seen a dead person, Mum?' and 'How can you tell when a person is dead?' Karen spilled a cup of tea on Gran's things and Mum, exasperated, ordered her to flush the goldfish down the toilet. Karen wishes *she* (Karen herself) were dead. Before the fatal plunge, though, Goldie (the spirit of the goldfish) appeared to Karen as a life-size girl punk.

Mr De Ath appeared, an undertaker wearing a lily in his lapel. The lily, we were told, was the thing to watch out for, the personal logo that identified its wearer or bearer as Death in disguise. His appearance had been triggered off by Karen's casual death wish. But he announced his mission was to 'gather' Gran. With compulsive flippancy he said he intended to make her 'kick the bucket'. Disarmingly he confessed it was 'a dog's life, being Death', to which Goldie retorted: 'You're breaking our hearts.' Death, with a snigger, clumsily capped it: 'I wish I was!' Death next revealed that he could do with either Goldie or Karen to make up his quote for the day. Goldie pleaded that Karen be allowed to choose the manner of her death. This was strongish meat for the audience who were, at this point, themselves as silent as the grave. After persuasion, Death agrees to use a bomb. The ideas was part of Goldie's delaying tactics, since she knew that all she and Karen had to do was lose themselves in a crowd and Death would not dare to make an attempt on their lives for fear of killing too many and thereby exceeding his quota. Death addresses the audience: 'Ugh! Kids! You're always causing trouble.' Flattered they responded with a hearty laugh.

The two friends then set about making plans to save Goldie. An aquarium, that's what they needed. Then Death's only chance would be to bomb Karen. The stage became a pet-shop with the actors impersonating snakes, lizards, parrots – and the audience showed visible admiration for their histrionic talents. But the shop proved unsafe as there was a marauding cat – called Lily! Confusing for the audience, as it later transpired, was the fact that Goldie had to be both inside and outside a plastic bag. Anyway, the goldfish got transferred to a bucket and taken on a bus (simulated brilliantly by the other actors).

The kids did seem to care a little about Goldie's safety at this point. Where to now? A lake in the park – the ideal hiding place for her.

On the way they met a woman conjuror, who tried to tempt Goldie (the person, now) to take up the trade. 'Would you like to be a conjuror?' she asked. 'Oh, yeah', answered Goldie, 'Sleight of fin and all that'. Deafening non-reaction from the children. Amid dire warnings to the audience about taking things from strangers, Goldie started to succumb to the offer of a sandwich – on a plate with a lily pattern – but disaster was averted and our heroine escaped.

A carnival occurred with a beautifully dressed 'Sun and Moon', dancing around, marking the progress of time. Karen had until midnight to save Goldie. It crossed her mind that Death might be kidding. Threatened by a yob (in charge of an arcade) she ran away. Goldie got into a 'helpful' car and it knocked down the fleeing Karen. (With a registration number of LIL 1, it is hardly surprising.)

Karen woke in hospital, the very one where Gran had been taken. Gran herself now appeared in Karen's head and ironically rejuvenated. Her body was in the operating theatre. Gran declared her willingness to pass away. Karen protested that it did not seem fair that people have to die. Karen and we were subjected to some moralising about death, about how necessary it was, how the world would be packed out if nobody left it. She herself then made a spectacular exit:

KAREN: You know, Gran – all the time Goldie and me were running away from Death.

GRAN: You can run away the day you're born, it's

natural, but all the time you're running straight towards it.

KAREN: Yeh. But I never realised you *wanted to go with Death* – neither did Death.

GRAN: These doctors, bless their hearts. They keep fighting death off.

[A surgeon enters, masked]

SURGEON: Excuse me.

GRAN: See. Come to drag me back to the operating table, have you?

SURGEON: I was wondering, miss, if I might have the pleasure of this dance.

GRAN: You cunning old lovable – fox.

KAREN: Gran – that's the doctor.

GRAN: Doctor, my eye! Certainly, I should be delighted.

So Gran was 'gathered' – *and* Goldie, it seemed. It turned out that the daily ration of deaths was a trick. 'A girl can't be too careful of that trick. Or a boy.' I imagine it was saying don't be too smug. Goldie was returned by the girl in the arcade – the Goldie in the bucket, that is.

What, in the end, did this performance seem to mean to these kids? Karen and Goldie successfully escaped death and won the kids' approval in doing this, so that Gran's acceptance of death came a bit pat and did not obviously relate to Karen's own case or that of the children. The personification of Death as a surgeon could convey an unfortunate, if unintended message! In Albee's *The Sandbox*, with which *Dead Easy* has some interesting similarities, Death is a wholesome young man, and Albee's Gran's delight in escaping with Death from life is more comprehensible, perhaps.

The actors engaged in a short discussion afterwards with some hit-or-miss questions. 'Did you like Goldie?' General 'Yeah!' 'Did you like Death?' 'No' 'Why not?' 'Cos he makes you die.' It looked as if the personified Death had done little to make the fact of death more palatable, to one child at least. Another question: 'Did you realise Goldie, the girl, was also the fish in the bag? Who did?' About half the hands went up. 'Who didn't?' The other half went up. 'Why not?' 'Cos it was stoopid!' Perhaps Common Stock, with *The Goldfish Bowl*, did better by showing their goldfish, Lola, at full size straight away.

To bring out into the open for small children a topic normally avoided was a brave and laudable aim, but I felt this play was – in the end – with its self-conscious flippancy, too conscientiously reassuring. The simple staging, the bright sunlight, the changing of roles and the sallies among the people in themselves provided a salutary distancing in helping remind the audience that what they were witnessing was only theatre.

The language, as in *Changing Gear*, sometimes drew attention to its own arch toughness with expressions such as 'dumb', 'thick', 'screwy', 'knuckle sandwich' and 'smack in the gob'. A slight loss of nerve all round, perhaps. The young audience attended politely enough, but their backward glances at the teachers made me wonder why.

I saw *The Arkansaw Bear* presented actually in America. It was performed by amateurs but I include it here because it tackles the same theme and the same problem as *Dead Easy* and there are some illuminating parallels to be drawn.

The story is about a girl, Tish, who is about to lose her grandfather through death and she protests and asks why he cannot live for ever. She is talking not to us but to Mother and Aunt Ellen who are and remain voices off-stage. Unable to face reality the girl runs away. On her travels she meets an Arkansaw Bear and a Mime (artist) who are also on the run, the Bear from death, the Mime from old age. A new arrival is Death himself in the form of a ring-master. The Bear seems to accept the fact that he is going to die (his name is in Death's book with the relevant date) and what he begs for is a respite to 'leave a foot print behind'. He is given the rest of the day to do this – until midnight. A new bear comes along, a young one. Why not teach him the act? All very well, but Death returns too soon. A friendly star – on whom you can wish – locks up Death in a tree, but only until dawn. The Arkansaw Bear teaches his dances to the new bear. On cue, Death comes out at dawn. Mime releases a symbolic balloon and the bear goes off to the great circus ring in the hereafter. What can happen to a Bear can happen to Grandad, we are meant to think. Tish is now reconciled to her impending bereavement.

The performance of 'The Arkansaw Bear' at New York University, by the Washington Square Players in conjunction with the Program in Educational Theatre, 8 March 1983

Although written for children, the play has some uncompromising and mature formulations on the inevitability and necessity of death. Unfortunately it repeats and hammers this *ad nauseam*, and, although there is humour in the script, the overall impression (especially with this production) was of a portentous parable. The dramatic action is fairly skimpy. The Bear accepts well before the end that he is going to die. In *Dead Easy*, we did not know about Gran's resignation until the last scene; focusing on Karen and Goldie, we were able to experience some anxiety on their behalf as they strove to dodge the mortal blow. In *The Arkansaw Bear* the tension was dependent on our concern as to whether the Bear was going to achieve a satisfactory death; that is to say, achieve a state of acceptance through having made a contribution to human society. I suspect coming to terms with the fact of death was a difficult enough problem for these youngsters without having to worry about leaving a footprint behind. The particular set of actors seemed to me incapable of projecting fear or panic as the fatal hour approached or desperation into the hurry to train the new dancing bear. The dancing lessons bored the restless audience. The Arkansaw Bear was presented sentimentally, but he proved less lovable and missable to me than the Great Bear in *Hiawatha*, where humour was the order of the day.

The setting was a proscenium arch university theatre. The auditorium was plunged in Stygian gloom. No audience participation *à la* Brian Way was expected or demanded. This was not a bad thing in itself, but on this occasion I felt that more interaction of some kind with the audience might have helped. The setting itself showed a pretty countryside and was lit in pantomimic colours. One was reminded, though, that it is not the British pantomime that pervades American drama for children, but Disney *et al*. Tish had a Dorothy-like pigtail out of *The Wizard of Oz*, and there was a cosy, shining star offering to grant wishes and sitting on a swing. Although the script does not shy away from reality this presentation had the effect of working against it. The images lacked power. The symbolic release of a balloon made the act of dying look easy – even twee. Then there was the great circus ring in the beyond that awaited the Bear. Not oblivion. And why a bear at all? A cuddly image in itself? It was interesting that we never saw Grandad as we saw Gran in *Dead Easy*. The Bear did duty for him. Death was an emblematic figure played by a black actor. (I was assured he also played the Bear on other occasions!)

There was talk from time to time of 'the joy and wonder of being alive', a salutary counterweight expressed by the Bear, but there was little theatrical exhilaration, little celebration in the event – or, at least, in this one. The children, brought in from schools, were quiet, but they were very unsophisticated and inexperienced as far as theatre was concerned. The novelty value could have worked in this production's favour, then.

For playwrights to tackle death head-on as a subject for children requires some courage, and to affirm the value of life in the face of that can be more difficult than to assert that social and political reform will change everything for the better.

Charlie and the Chocolate Factory, by Ronald Dahl, is an original fantasy in story form. Its huge popularity was bound to tempt someone to adapt it for stage if only for the fact that it would pull in an audience. Timothy Raison did it for the English Touring Company and it went on tour directed by the celebrated Mike Bradwell.

Five youngsters win a tour of Willy Wonka's fantastic chocolate factory; four selfish ones receive fitting punishments and the one good one receives the factory itself. A major problem for an adaptor is the shortage of dramatic action and a bewildering succession of exotic locations. Raison tried – with peripheral effect – to beef up the plot by adding a villain, a business rival who is really Grandpa in disguise, having been engaged by Wonka to tempt all five kids to steal an everlasting gobstopper. Charlie alone chooses loyalty to the firm but it is at the risk of losing house and Grandad, a small price to pay! The moral ambiguity of Wonka himself is skated over.

When I caught up with the production in Sheffield I saw

a performance in which the cast attacked the piece with energy and versatility, but Mike Bradwell's direction went for a knockabout, pantomimic style and the 'villain', identified by his ugly appearance and a green light, was robbed of any real sense of threat. The play was presented on a single transportable set and effective use was made of back projection, lighting and sound. But the production resorted to familiar and weary participation routines to get the audience involved. There was music, of course, and some of the numbers were good and lively. One, though, recorded Charlie's sententious commitment to his 'soul' and 'conscience'. It made me appreciate the real seriousness of intention that lay behind *Dead Easy* and *The Arkansaw Bear*.

Fantasy is the most popular mode for children's plays in East Germany, particularly in the form of fairy-tales or *Märchen*. This might seem surprising in a country where one might expect no opportunity to be lost to reinforce socialist education. However, with a little ingenuity, even politically neutral material can made to deliver a political message, and an adventitious choice of story can be made to seem deliberate

I saw a play called *Der Vogelkopp* (Bird-head) by Albert Wendt, performed at the Theater der Freundschaft in East Berlin in 1987. The story given in the programme was as follows (the translation is my wife's).

The Queen of this country is exceptionally wise. Her late husband, with foolish zeal, persecuted all the unusual people in the kingdom and shut them up in schools to drive out their obstinacy. The Queen repudiates this policy and prefers a more just regime. Therefore she takes an interest in these special people and can no longer reject their talents. Every year she organises an Odd Fellows' Festival so as to get to know them.

This year, she is expecting a new guest, Vogelkopp. Her curiosity is aroused by the fact that Vogelkopp never takes his cap from his head. Actually, the reason for this is that he keeps a nest of young birds under his cap to protect them from the cold. He was driven out of Hats-Off Street because he disregarded the law and did not raise his cap. His wife declared him to be mad and sued for a divorce. Even in front of the Queen's throne his birds mean more to him than royal favour. Through the machinations of an Under-Secretary he finds himself faced with execution. When the secret comes out, the soft-hearted executioner cannot bear to risk harming the birds with his axe. The Queen dismisses the Under-Secretary and takes Vogelkopp for her new king.

Of central importance is the scene at the festival where Bird-head meets other 'Odd Fellows'. Fred, the swinger, swings across the stage on a chandelier, enjoying the sheer pleasure of movement. Old Look-you-in-the-Eye has a gift of insight into people. The Specialist passionately examines the effect of different words so as to use them appropriately in whatever context. Give-away is a compulsive shedder of possessions. The learned Professor goes around with a dummy in his mouth.

The play, I was told, reflected current Party thinking on the need for more individualism in society. Vogelkopp was prepared to die to defend the birds, to give his life to save life. I think the birds would have had a dicey future once his head was off. It was difficult to get from the Odd Fellows a sense of the political importance of the individual conscience. As played, they roused a lot of laughter and came over as harmless eccentrics. The professor's dummy was supposed to signify that he retained his childlike curiosity, according to the programme note, but I doubt that particular message came over. The production did make use of some stylised devices. The three birds were played by three girls who kept popping up. In *Dead Easy*, youngsters in the audience failed to relate the girl playing the goldfish to the life-size goldfish in the plastic bag, but the children watching *Vogelkopp* were sophisticated enough to have no trouble with the twin locations.

Old King Cole

Ken Campbell, whose Road Shows were popular in the pub circuit of the adult 'fringe', brings his quirky, individual fantasies to the world of children's theatre. His antecedents are the comics *Beano* and *Dandy*, Spike Milligan and Laurel and Hardy. Rosalind Asquith calls him 'the virtuoso of the absurd'[5] and Aidan Chambers 'the fashion-setting arch clown of one prevailing mood'.[6] In *Asterix* he transfers the characters from the famous comics straight to the stage, grotesquely costumed and larger than life. Through them and the stories of Romans and Gauls, he debunks romantic and heroic posturing and exposes some of the ridiculous elements in political manoeurvering. Aidan Chambers, wanting to claim Campbell for Literature, stresses the delight in verbal invention, and Asquith his sensitive awareness of the 'logic of nonsense'.[7] The verbal formulations in *Asterix*, though, sometimes require the political sophistication of adults to appreciate the satirical point. Chambers also credits Campbell with having deeply personal reasons for his theatrical preoccupations. 'There is an innocence and vulnerability about all of Campbell's work; reading or watching it one feels that the clowning is really a way to hide and to keep at bay a terrible fear of a puzzling, untrustworthy world.'[8]

Skungpoomery and *Old King Cole* feature Faz and twoo, the zany inventor and his feeble-minded assistant. *Skungpoomery* contains Campbell vocabulary such as 'bunkjamjarmering – smearing strawberry jam on your pyjamas and doing a bunk into the street'. *Old King Cole* was written for Peter Cheesman, the adventurous director of the Victoria Theatre (in the round) at Stoke-on-Trent in 1968. Campbell takes as his focus the two comic robbers who are allocated only a small part in the traditional pantomime. I produced the play at the University of Sheffield Drama Studio in 1983, and because I can speak of it very much from the inside, I propose to treat it in a proportionately larger amount of detail, saying something about the evolution of the production through rehearsals, the kind of demands it made on actors and director and the difference it made to it to expose it to particular audiences. The proportion of attention paid is not an indication of its superior significance as an example of children's theatre.

The play opens in the office of the Amazing Faz and his feeble-minded assistant, twoo. Faz is an inventor who puts his ingenuity to the service of 'dirty deeds'. twoo has a large overcoat with huge pockets from which he can, and does, produce almost anything at will. Rats have been nibbling at Faz's sausages and he invents a rat-trap to lure the rat on with a flying sausage (actually it is on a string). But they trap not a rat but weedy Baron Wadd, who has come in reply to an advertisement put by Faz in the local paper. The Baron says he wants to marry the princess Daphne, daughter of Old King and Old Queen Cole, but the King has decreed that Daphne shall marry the winner of a sports competition at Wembley Stadium. The Baron is no 'sporto' but Cyril, the King's new fiddler, is. The Baron pleads with Faz to undermine Cyril's performance so as to allow the Baron to win and he promises Faz that he shall have a large reward and a friend at court. Faz agrees to do it and declares that he and twoo will come disguised as track officials and find ways of incapacitating Cyril.

At Wembley Stadium a pompous Master of Ceremonies announces a best-of-nine-event contest before the royal party. In the royal party, the Queen is hard put to control the cheeky behaviour of and constant demands from her daughter. Daphne soon conceives an attraction towards one of the track officials, and the official, twoo, reciprocates. The dirty tricks are perpetrated but keep misfiring because of the Baron's incompetence. The first event is boxing but the Baron cannot lift his glove (metal-weighted by Faz). Cyril, the super-fit bighead, is awarded the first point. In the egg-and-spoon race, one egg is taped to the spoon but the Baron picks the wrong one. He also picks the wrong – the limp and 'doctored' – sword for the sword-fight, muddled by his inability to remember the sort of mnemonic chant that Danny Kaye failed to get right in *The Court Jester*. His chant may be meaningless but it is rhythmical and the characters are tempted into dancing, Daphne with twoo. For this she earns a sharp rebuke from her mother. The dance only stops when Old King Cole puts his foot down, metaphorically. Daphne declares that the basis of her interest in twoo is his abililty to supply all her wants from his mysterious pockets, especially lollipops. Order restored, the time comes for the duck-shooting event, in which the contestant has to fire at a passing duck. According to Faz's plan, when the Baron misses his duck, as he surely will, twoo will throw one from his pocket on to the ground. The trouble is that twoo's duck is seen to be a toy one. The MC puts it to the vote among the audience as to whether the Baron's duck should count and the audience, as expected, will vote in favour of the Baron.

In a wonderfully comic sequence, Cyril now takes his turn and has his bead drawn on a real duck. Just as he is about to fire, twoo creeps up behind him and yanks his shorts down, revealing bright red pants. Cyril's gun wavers and puts a bullet up the backside of Faz, as he bends to tie his shoelace. With a yell, Faz sets off on a rapid tour of the stadium followed by twoo with a bucket of water. Daphne, observing Cyril's red pants, offers their colour as another good reason for her not to marry him.

At the archery, twoo sticks an arrow into the outer ring of Cyril's target but the Baron shoots Faz through the hat. Cyril is declared the overall winner of the contest and, to her chagrin, Daphne must be married to him now, pants and all. Cyril protests that though he won her he does love her too. Old King Cole invites everybody to the wedding.

In the palace next morning, it is nearly time for the wedding. Faz, twoo and the Baron contemplate the use of the ultimate weapon, 'paraphernalia', which is kept in an intriguing suitcase. But Faz doubts it will work on a 'sporto' like Cyril. They will have to daze him first. A large box walks on, seen to move only by twoo and the audience. Faz proceeds with the planning and proposes to use the Messy Clothes Wag Trap. For this they will need a washing-machine, bubble mixture, a pint of oil, two pulley wheels, a mountaineering rope and clips and a ton weight. The items that even twoo cannot produce will have to be found. To twoo is delegated the task of looking for a washing-machine, while Faz and the Baron look for a ton weight. Before twoo can leave the room, as Faz and the Baron have just done, Daphne pops out of the box. She reveals she wants to marry twoo (he being too dim to have already surmised as much). twoo admits he would rather like that, especially if there is no 'soppy kissing', but he flees when Daphne chases him with the intention of finding out the secret of his pockets.

There is a comic episode next when the royal couple and Cyril come looking for Daphne. She and twoo are hiding in the box, and the royals and Cyril are touched up when they stand by it and each, of course, blames the others. Alone again, twoo and Daphne make a plan of their own to hold up the wedding party with pistols and demand the right to marry each other. Faz and the Baron return, and with complicated business the washing-machine is prepared and the ton weight hung in position overhead nearby. With the audience's expected connivance, Cyril is called over to them (the audience), blown back, slips on the oil and messes up his clothes, is advised to strip and put his clothes into the washing machine. twoo pops out, Cyril staggers back in surprise and twoo looses the rope (which is anchored to the washing-machine). The weight lands on Cyril and knocks him 'umpy doodly'. The royal party arrives, but their plans are thwarted by the sudden eruption of paraphernalia which, in an amazing scene, has everybody whirling around trance-like as lights go on and off, weird sounds wail away and objects fly hither and thither. It is a totally disorientating experience; chaos is come again. Immediately it finishes, twoo and Daphne (who have not been affected) stand there brandishing pistols. But the king suddenly becomes *compos mentis* again and assumes an air of authority and control, and he calmly disarms Daphne and delivers a little homily on the inappropriateness of force. He then demonstrates the inappropriateness of democracy by calling on the audience to vote to decide whether twoo and Daphne are to be married. (Nobody questions the method, of course.) The result is predictable and twoo is dubbed Duke. He has abandoned his coat and Faz and Baron Wadd are left alone with it. Faz is sad at the loss of his sidekick but the Baron proposes that he takes twoo's place in the partnership. It is presumed the audience will endorse the decision.

The script appealed to me on a number of counts. It is very inventive, particularly on the level of incident and physical action but to some extent verbally. (Cyril is knocked 'umpy-doodly' and the protagonists 'fiendish' about. There is a verb 'to sausage' and 'paraphernalia' acquires new and menacing overtones.) It explores the comic potential of experience. Although it contains material ripe for sentimental pantomime treatment, such as the fact that Daphne is being forced to wed somebody her domineering mother lays on for her, Daphne seems well able to take care of herself. twoo, the underdog, surprises his partner, Faz, by counterplotting. In fact it is not by being good that twoo and Daphne triumph, but by being one step ahead in a world of selfish connivers. Daphne's motives are selfish; twoo has some sort of affinity for the bullied girl. Cyril plangently cries: 'I love you, Daphne!' to the unresponsive princess, but Cyril, although physically the nearest thing to Prince Charming that we have, is such a bighead that it is difficult to sympathise with him too much. There is some reference to politics at the end when Old King Cole denounces violence and proposes a democratic vote, but the tongue remains firmly in the cheek and at least the play does not become heavy.

The structure is tight and clear. The plot is actually *about* plotting and Campbell writes with clarity, spelling each stage out to the audience without patronising them. Sometimes the deliberateness is justified by the fact that it is twoo who is trying to take it in. The audience can thus be helped to understand and at the same time feel superior to the feeble-minded listener onstage. The use of the MC in the Wembley Stadium scene is a clever device and his pomposity contrasts with the undignified events he is commenting on.

The play starts slowly and quietly as the foundations are laid in terms of plot and personalities, but this leaves plenty of room for it to hot up and build towards the release of paraphernalia in Scene 3. The kids are requested to help – in the trapping of a rat, or of Cyril, for instance – but one never feels the play needs the audience's permission to continue. In *Old King Cole* it is all part of a conspiracy of high spirits. Sometimes the audience's support is solicited for a particular character (for example the Baron), but there is some latitude as to whether he gets it, some autonomy allowed to the audience.

Campbell hits the level of development and sophistication of the audience pretty accurately. Intended for children of primary-school age, it offers a release from everyday reality into anarchy; it approves of mischief-making and it allows them to laugh at the farcical violence that occurs to Faz's foot, hand and backside (shades of Oliver Hardy). But nobody who does not deserve to be hurt actually suffers from it in the end. Faz is a victim of fate. Daphne and twoo sidestep the sexual by repudiating any 'soppy kissing' in their marriage. The comedy debunks the pompous and the smug.

There is some appeal to the nostalgia of middle-aged parents in the *Beano* and *Dandy* world that Campbell creates. Some directors claim that there are a number of *double entendres* deliberately built into the script which are addressed to the adults in the audience. I do not know what Campbell himself intended, but, as written, the script seems to me to require a careful respect for children rather than a sniggering betrayal. Lines which could (illegitimately, in my eyes) be milked for ambiguous delivery are, for example, Daphne's declaration that she wants to marry twoo in order to find out the secret of his pockets which, she believes, contain 'everything I ever want'. These two want no soppy kissing, so the argument goes, because they want more than that. The string in the rat-trap goes from the 'dangle to the up position', the Baron's sword wilts like a symbol of his general impotence, the fiddlers are called 'John, Thomas and Cyril', and there is much prodding between twoo and Daphne. But I would maintain that Campbell has written us a play and not a pantomime.

The rehearsals of 'Old King Cole'

We had about six weeks to rehearse the play. I chose to perform it in traverse, although this would load a lot of responsibility on to the actors, their voices and bodies unaided by a beguiling set. It would help to achieve intimacy with the audience, hopefully, and be very useful when different sections of the audience made different contributions.

Early rehearsals were taken up with exploring character and getting the feel of the play and its style. The cast were very apprehensive about playing to small children but were intrigued by the challenge:

- Bob, playing Faz, was very inventive and made good suggestions about practicalities. He did need to take the audience with him more.
- Richard, as twoo, was obsessed with the search for a voice. Eventually Mummerset worked the best for him. He was worried about being a bit tall for twoo.

He was a bit quiet in his manner of playing and needed to be more out-front and obvious.

- Ray, as Cyril, was a more strident actor, more self-confident. A bit too nice and lovable at the moment, more so than the Baron (unfortunately).
- Adrian, as the Baron, was worried about making the Baron either too pathetic or too much of pain in the backside. Cultivated a comic ditheriness but would need to vary his style of movement at times. Needed to build the 'fiendish' side, the sniggering side a bit more.
- Bill, as MC, needed to find his own best position on the stage for his commentary on the contest. Spoke too fast. Found it hard to marry his directions with what he was supposed to be commenting on. Perhaps the commentary could *follow* what happens at times, rather than 'steering' it.
- Joan, as Queen, was too gentle. Needed to be more of a virago, if the audience were to sympathise with the naughty and selfish Daphne (Helen).
- Peter, as Old King Cole, was too ponderous at the moment. Out of key with the rest. The royal party needed some special treatment. It was difficult in traverse to keep them in the minds of the audience. Would need to try to involve them more where possible, giving their reactions more prominence without making them too eye catching.

The acting, on the whole, was too vigorous: my fault for demanding energy. Wanted a sense of momentum, so started 'over the top' rather than underplaying, as being the easier extreme to move away from. The result was a passable peak reached too early. Needed now to concentrate on varying the pace, improving the timing, stopping the headlong rush and analysing the episodes for effectiveness and clarity. Could try some 'frozen' pictures. After the first few sessions, I began to worry that the play might become a set of comic antics with no involving storyline and be played at the same level all the time. Some of the cast agree.

I told them I had heard that the play could be deadly boring and that I was anxious at all costs to avoid that. Campbell wanted it to have the appeal of a thriller!

I tried playing it at a more naturalistic level, bringing out the following characteristics:

- Faz: his desperation to succeed; his fondness for and exasperation with twoo.
- twoo: well meaning; a victim but resilient; not a *total* fool.
- Cyril: more of a revolting bighead.
- Baron: anxious to succeed, ambitious, unscrupulous and incompetent.
- King: wanted to retain some semblance of authority; civilised person.
- Queen: wanted her daughter to toe the line and marry well.
- Daphne: did not want to be tamed; rejoiced in being silly and unconventional.

We would hope the audience would sympathise with twoo as a victim, butt and anarchist; Daphne because she was rude to authority; Faz because he was 'fiendish' and ingenious but a victim also, this time of fate, and lonely at the end. He would need to find a way of playing the end which was genuine but not tear-jerking. Definitely should not send it up.

There was a general worry about what would 'go' with a very young audience. Was 'going' to be the criterion? Might there be the temptation of 'going' for an easy laugh?

The fifth rehearsal was a depressing affair, and only partly because I did not feel up to it. Did a desultory run-through of Scene 2, the Wembley scene. Already it had become mechanical with the MC butting in before his cues, and the Baron and Cyril anticipating the next development. Delivered my pep-talk about the need to emphasise the storyline and the motivations but to little effect. Must be more specific and detailed next time. We tried the end of the play, the paraphernalia episode, but it was very difficult in practical terms. I let it run, with crazed characters reeling about, to see what happened spontaneously. Then had to plot it more positively; paradoxically, the effect of disorder needed the order of art to be effective. To diversify the 'madness', I gave each an animal noise to make. Also gave them individual rhythms and tempos in their movement within an overall clockwise sweep of the acting area. Needed to hold a balance between their creative offerings and the discipline of the ensemble.

Bob was having difficulties with Faz and was making me a bit edgy by his constant protests and his proposals for cutting. He was worried that Faz was becoming too nasty and delivering too many blows to twoo. Richard (twoo) and Peter (the King) were having difficulties swallowing their embarrassment and making animal noises. Adrian (the Baron) was proving at this point a bit over-loquacious and would need to be squashed, perhaps. I concluded that I had been a bit too democratic and had encouraged protests and alternative suggestions without spelling it out that I was ultimately responsible for what was and was not accepted. However, when useful creativity was involved, it gave the actors a stake in the performance.

Had a row with Bob about his introducing and overloading projected interplay with the audience on the 'Oh, yes he did. Oh, no he didn't' level. We discussed 'participation'. Bob wanted to find an excuse to bring the kids on to the stage in Scene 3, but I put my foot down. The play seemed to have enough built-in opportunities for audience 'help' already, and the play does turn against Faz and the Baron in the end.

Fourth week. End of play still presenting problems. Paraphernalia tending to swamp the plot – the holding-up of Cyril and the rescue of Daphne. Peter (the King) was currently so concerned with aping Prince Charles that his lines were indistinguisable. They *all* needed to project more, now. Having gone through the phase of individualism, the time was now ripe to concentrate on the team, the ensemble and the overall effect of the play. I needed to remind them of the story again. I needed to let the best effects, the best intonations for trigger lines crystallise. I discovered that the music recordist had not read the play! Richard (twoo) felt in need of advice on how to play in a half-mask, track-official disguise in Scene 2. His performance seemed very expressive to me as it was. Bill's mike had a trailing flex so we decided to substitute a wire-less one.

The plot line and motives getting lost again. Stressed the essential selfishness and greed of most of the characters. Cyril was quite moving when he declared his love to Daphne but he shouldn't be. I encouraged Ray to send him up a bit. Audience mustn't like him too much as they might not help to trap him. Discussed the end of the play, where twoo gets Daphne and Faz gets the Baron. In what way was it artistically 'right'? If it wasn't right as written was there anything in performance we could do? Did the play support the political status quo – aristocracy and all that? Faz was motivated by money yet his rejection by twoo could be rather sad. Does comedy need a threat of sadness or danger? People do lose friends and we wanted to be truthful to the kids. Faz did bounce back, after all. Realised the Baron becomes more sympathetic at the end on account of his *concern* for Faz.

Dreadful run-through. Lack of concentration, partly through boredom and familiarity. Laughing at the play, curiously enough like mischievous kids. I read the riot act and took the cast to task for insulting the potential audience. The performance had to be, in an important sense, *serious*. The example of twoo could reassure those in the audience, for instance, who were considered 'daft' by their peers as well as winning over the peers.

Just before the performance, the production improved greatly. I felt the cast had at last acquired a viable approach, with the confidence to improvise and change within acceptable limits in adjustment to whatever might occur in the theatre.

The performances of 'Old King Cole' in the Sheffield University Drama Studio

In performance, the traverse setting worked well and there was a good deal of spontaneous participation and enthusiastic, almost desperate advice. The actors had to work hard to earn legitimate sympathy, though, and the varying composition of the audiences forced continual adjustment on their part. One audience consisted of semi-delinquent members of family groups who threw things at Cyril. They themselves ranged freely and unchecked about the auditorium and to the rail of the balcony. There were school parties large enough to avoid teacher domination and, on one occasion, rather inhibited, uniformed girls. Sometimes there was a large adult contingent (including academics) and laughter came at unexpected moments.

The first act, the rat-catching scene, tended to be received quietly, and Faz, twoo and the Baron had to make absolutely sure that the small children were taken step by step through the exposition and the plotting. There was always the danger of losing attention during more verbal sections and the vigorous use of gesture by the actors became a condition of survival. On all occasions, the temperature rose fairly rapidly with the Wembley scene and sometimes we got absolute uproar when Cyril was pronounced the winner. There was some genuine division of sympathy and the production left the audience the autonomy to express it. I think the legal justice of the outcome was not really questioned, though. The adults seemed to be getting some enjoyment over and above that of seeing their offspring happy. The potentially suggestive bits were spotted and sometime responded to, but I am still sure that a director should not *play* for them behind the youngsters' backs. Interestingly there were other parts which had a special appeal for adults. There was the adoption by Peter (the King) of the habit of referring to Daphne as 'one's daughter' and his Noel Coward delivery of his patriotic speech, 'This is Great Britain . . . '; twoo guilelessly pointing out and emphasising (Laurel-like) the fact that the embarrassed Faz's book had not sold any copies at all; there was twoo's obvious conclusion that there must be somebody in the walking box (which merely spoke the minds of the youngest, though). The MC says that Cyril is 'looking to see if he can see a duck' and the adults appreciated the deliberate obviousness of the dramatic logic.

It was pronounced an enjoyable production by young and old alike, and the fact that it was – in the end – a labour of love for the actors communicated itself to the spectators. Perhaps, as Aidan Chambers is moved to say, children 'can be an appreciative audience for stronger meat than is often served up in plays specially for them',[9] but there is a place for *Old King Cole* and its like when it can throw genuine light on an area of human experience, however limited that area might be.

6
'Social Realism' and Plays Based on Political Issues

Although fantasy plays may successfully explore political issues (for example the dramatised version of *Animal Farm* at the National), the most popular mode for the enterprise is 'social realism'. The phrase can be misleading, as it can imply a preoccupation with the sordid at the expense of more attractive sides of 'reality'. In this context, though, it is taken to mean a more literal rendering of the world of social experience. Such are the connotations of fantasy that some companies, perhaps, believe that a 'literalist' style might seem to signal a more 'relevant' play and have a better chance of being taken seriously.

Overwhelmingly the kind of theatre that takes as its priority the exploration of social and political issues is the product of TIE and YPT companies. Usually the artists start from a committed standpoint and politically this is generally left-wing. Commitment, as I have observed, is in itself no bad thing, although *artistic* success depends on whether the mind of the creator is a closed or an open

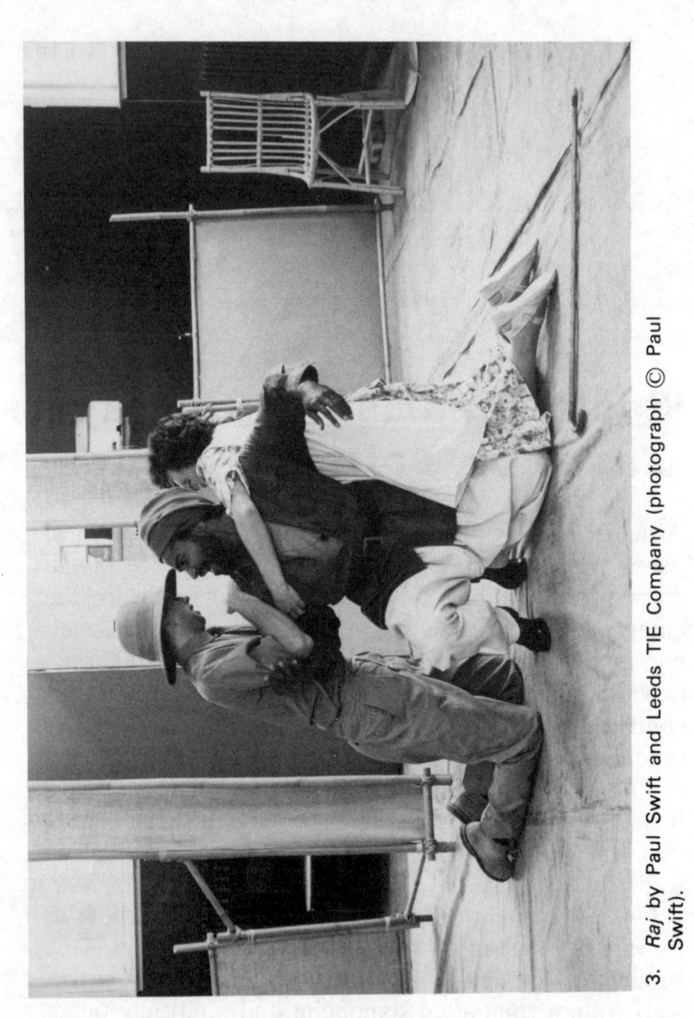

3. *Raj* by Paul Swift and Leeds TIE Company (photograph © Paul Swift).

one. Sometimes this kind of theatre may express a corporate view of an ensemble committed to social and political change. SCYPT, and particularly a nucleus within it of members of the Workers' Revolutionary Party, has set the seal of approval on the use of theatre for political ends, although there have been dissentient voices.[1]

In the 1980s, there was plenty of political change in the air. It just did not happen to be the kind of political change YPT companies found congenial. This too influenced the stance of some of them. Some were tempted even more to go beyond the educational (artistic?) goal of raising political consciousness to the goal of recommending left-wing solutions. Some with the potent threat of censorship hanging over them, succumbed to defeatism. Les Smith, 1983, talked of companies 'opting out of disruption' and of a current atmosphere of 'stasis', a sapping of the will to resist and a feeling of 'helplessness in the face of social decay'.[2] They might go for less risky plays offering useful practical instruction.

TIE and YPT were not unresponsive to developments in the adult fringe and some, like Pam Schweitzer, would hold that:

> In order to demonstrate that seven-year-olds can rise to an intellectual challenge and participate in debate on issues which the company themselves think are important and exciting, TIE teams have pioneered innovatory forms of programme-devising, staging and actor–audience relationship which might well prove significant for other branches of the theatre.[3]

And, of course, there were community theatre groups that took the same play into different venues. Writers like Edward Bond wrote for young people, and young people's plays were given an airing in studios open to the general public. Well-known fringe groups like Paynes Plough experimented with multi-media presentations. The Royal Shakespeare Company staged David Edgar's adaptation of *Nicholas Nickleby* which made the sort of free use of narrator that Shared Experience had done. There was a proliferation of small touring companies, usually formed by the recent products of universities, polytechnics and colleges of higher education. Some called themselves TIE groups, although the members' experience of teaching may have been limited and unhappy. They were responsible for interesting formal experiment, though, and some earned Arts Council support.

With political theatre for young people, the theme is the most important factor, and the theatres tackled many of the burning issues of their time, such as women's rights, racialism, the police, the treatment of disability and class. Sometimes these companies chose a more exotic setting (historically or geographically). Some plays got published – by Methuen and Amber Lane Press, for example. Some sank into oblivion; some were passed on in typescript from company to company.

In 1983, York YPT mounted a play called *Better in the Long Run*. It was about unemployment and it was devised by the company with Chris Wallis, the director, coming in at a later stage to tidy up the product. Russ, one of the actors, did an overall draft and other actors worked on different sections. The play was very patchy and the parts that Russ worked on in detail were markedly sharper, more ironic and sardonic than the others. Russ said there was the temptation, working this way, to settle for the lowest common denominator. These were 'short-stay' actors in the main, who had not remained together long enough to gel as an ensemble.

Russ joined the group for political reasons. His commitment to socialist change was strong and this must have fired his contributions. But while he was happy about the content, he was unhappy about the play as a play. Top priority was given to the message (the need 'do something' about unemployment). The characters were two-dimensional embodiments of publicly induced attitudes. Certainly one did not get the sense of their having much personal life. Perhaps this might not have mattered so much if the dialogue had not been flat, banal and cliché-ridden and the situations lacking in dramatic tension. Chris Wallis described the play as 'low key' and he was right. Interest was angled for by surface devices rather than organic form.

Better in the Long Run was about two girls, punky Sharon and middle-class Clare and their families. Briefly, Sharon progressed via the Youth Opportunities Programme and a confrontation with her establishment-supporting army boyfriend to enlightenment (knowing the 'message' of the play). Clare was all set for her A level examinations at school. She discovered that her own father had been thrown out of work but had not told his wife. She was about to pack in her A level course when Sharon, of all people, urged her to stick to her A level ambitions and get wisdom. Nothing wrong with a hopeful ending as such. Walter Greenwood, though, in *Love on the Dole* demonstrated that a play conveying an overwhelmingly hopeless sense of being trapped can be equally disturbing and convincing. The girls belonged to the Harriers Club at the beginning of *Better in the Long Run* but at the end both gave up running as a hobby.

The performance of 'Better in the Long Run' at Ashfield Secondary School, York, by York Young People's Theatre Company, 2 February 1983

The play was staged in traverse with two screens, one at either end of the acting space. From time to time, the location that the space represented was signalled by a placard – in true Brechtian fashion.

There was a short, uninvolving exposition. The opening scenes showed the girls in their respective family milieux. Sharon unemployed still and Mother took a conventional attitude in telling her daughter that she had 'only herself to blame'. In Clare Fairfax's house, father peddled the Tory line that Clare must make her way by her own efforts. The A level grind was the route for her but she said she would never give up running (her hobby). Unfortunately no real passion for the running communicated itself to the audience.

Gary, the army boyfriend, entered Sharon's house. He represented a man with a job. The idea was planted that Gary was taking part in manoeuvres and that in his particular job he had to obey orders. Father entered the room and the play and complained that Sharon was not doing anything – even clearing up. The effects of unemployment? 'You think it's all going to be handed to you on a plate', he said. Sharon talked of a YOP (Youth Opportunities Programme) scheme and Father tried to push her to look for a proper job. 'Rule Britannia', played off-key, heralded a change of scene and made a ham-fisted comment. The radio announced that 'Sir Keith Joseph thinks the recession is bottoming out.' The irony was very blatant. Sharon's YOP scheme took her to the hospital laundry. A convenient teabreak allowed Sharon and a conveniently articulate workmate to discuss politics and to put a left-wing argument. Russ, as foreman, sniggered that YOPs kept wages down, with free labour and with the government paying the wages. Adding to the crude stereotyping, Mozart transported us to the Fairfax household. A long pause occurred which Mr Fairfax filled in with turning over the pages of his newspaper. The radio, with laboured irony, announced support for private and small firms by the Government. Mrs Thatcher, apparently, also said that the recession was bottoming out. At the hospital gates, hospital workers were on strike. Sharon was with the voluble women pickets, she having, as they said, 'learned fast'. All vital supplies were being stopped. A lorry driver inveighed against 'bloody unions' but turned back to cheers from the strikers and to an implication that the audience should feel a warm surge of support.

The scene moved to the 'John Bull' public house, where Gary was waiting to be called to action. The troops were to be pitted against the strikers. Plainly Gary had divided loyalties. In a confrontation with his girl friend, he finally took the official line and left her with the words: 'I'll see you when you come to your senses.' The dilemma was not really built up to, though. The actress playing Sharon came to life at this point but the scene fell short of strong dramatic conflict. Actually there were the elements of a good scene here but it needed better writing. Next there was a scene in the Social Manager's Office. Russ gave the part of 'social worker' an individual stamp, making him squeamish about using embarrassing words 'like . . . er . . . strike'. Sharon came up with an example of would-be racy dialogue: 'We're stuck in this bleeding great rut and all we want to do is claw our way out.' The Odeon Cinema next. Mr Fairfax arrived and met Clare there. She was curious as to why he was not at work, but the truth emerged that he had been jobless for a while and had been passing time in the cinema so as to fool his wife into thinking he was still doing his job. 'I just didn't believe it could happen to me', he said plaintively. In showing his human face he won some audience sympathy here. His wife, a teacher was of the opinion that those out of work do not *want* to work. The ethic 'work hard and you'll get on' was explicitly rubbished. Again, not a bad scene in conception. The final scene was in the Harriers Club. Clare and Sharon had gone off the idea of 'running' now. Clare had also gone off A levels, now realising what a waste of time it was. Sharon stepped in and told her that 'kicking out' did not get you anywhere. She urged Clare to 'channel' her anger. Clare should do her A levels and thereby get understanding. It was not clear how this would work and the advice came over just a little bit glib.

I do not think one could doubt the sincerity of those who devised the piece. To work as a play, though, it needed something more than an assumption that what it was showing was self-evidently true. The audience – in their mid-teens – were remarkably quiet. It could have been rivetted attention but I rather think it was because they had not been much stirred.

Later the same year (1983) Perspectives Theatre Company took on a tour of the district a programme entitled *Gaining Ground*. It consisted of a complete play of about an hour in length and a follow-up workshop lasting about an hour and half. A leaflet states its aims:

> The piece will be about the concerns and experiences of young unemployed or potentially unemployed people, with the purpose of reinforcing their sense of value and worth in a society that increasingly offers No Hope and No Future.

In other words, it tackles the same subject as *Better in the Long Run* but this time the play is intended for a 'community' audience. The company had great ambitions for the project although not all the issues and concerns they hoped to raise would have to be embodied in the play. Under 'The Content' were listed the following items:

1. The work ethic: does not having a 'job' mean you do not have a 'use' in Society?
2. How does the state of unemployment differ for those who have never worked since school and those who have been made redundant?
3. New training initiatives, YOP schemes and other government-sponsored programmes: how useful are they? How are they working on a local level? Are they a growth industry?
4. What is the TUC's present policy on youth unemployment and what are its effects?
5. What do young employed people think about trade unions and other traditional organisations in the Labour movement?
6. How do young people cope with life-on-the-dole? What are their aspirations? Is there any sense of 'Solidarity' or self-help between them?
7. Leisure: what can young people do with it? Is it really a time for self development and enjoyment or is it enforced idleness?
8. How does youth unemployment affect different classes? Will a degree still guarantee a job? How does youth employment affect the sexes? Is it different for girls?

The play had a designated writer, Paul Goetzee, who apparently made use of ideas suggested by the company as well as his own. The focus was on a group of youngsters who claimed a 'dump' for their 'ground'. Bell, in parti-coloured jeans and outrageous ear-rings, was pregnant by a disappearing boyfriend. Her friend, Cynth, in a respectable skirt, worked on a YOP scheme at the kennels where she was blissfully happy. Morg was fat and was a mad inventor type who trundled around a supermarket trolley with a CB radio attached and who nursed the ambition to put together a Cortina one day. Kev was Bell's brother who had been promised a fee of £2000 by the local factory owner to burn the factory down. The factory owner was cynical about the prospects of selling his factory and wanted the insurance money.

The performance of 'Gaining Ground' at the Valley Youth Centre, Worksop, by Perspectives Theatre Company, on the evening of 30 June 1983

The audience, a capacity one, but small in number, were in the main of early to mid teens. Observers such as myself were tolerated but it was obvious that the team preferred a homogeneous audience so as to build up an intimate relationship within which the workshop could flourish. The play opened with an intriguing banging noise coming from inside a corrugated iron screen folded into a box. It opened out to reveal Morg drumming on old oil cans. Opened not fully, the screen now represented factory gates. Red lights played over the scene and it was to this red light that we returned at the end of the play. Thus the light gave a foretaste of the fire without giving it away; the sort of bold theatrical touch missing from *Better in the Long Run*.

Prominent also onstage was a public phone-box. We saw Bell trying to get money out of brother Kev to finance an abortion. Her other condition, joblessness, threatened to make the abortion impossible. The phone rang and on the other end was a man who announced his intention of committing suicide because of being unemployed. Bell assumed responsibility for keeping up his morale. After he had unhelpfully hung up, she did this by means of Morg's CB Radio. The plot-contrivance stood out so stark that the young audience began giggling. In another creaking development, Morg found the petrol with which Kev was to burn down the factory and refused to hand it over or sell it. Cynth received a letter which, for a while, she shrank from opening. When she did, we learned that it informed her of her dismissal from the kennels. A moving moment for the character, executed with conviction by the actress but arousing mirth in the auditorium. A charitable explanation could be that the spectators were genuinely touched and laughed out of embarrassment. Gradually all the options closed for the young characters. The factory became the focus of their resentment. Even the potential suicide had been an employee there. Having established a state of general vengefulness, the play allowed the factory to be burned down by accident, but the message that came over was that any one of the unemployed would be prepared to burn down a factory. The play included some lighter moments such as when Morg made a car of out of the oil drums and there was the odd joke about the sexual exploits of Morg and Cynth, because, I suspect, that is the sort of thing teenagers get up to, or so the stereotyping would have us believe.

The play was really too short to evolve convincingly. The motivation was not particularly credible. Were they really all capable of arson (and forgivably so)? Or was there a touch of melodramatic overstatement and scaremongering? The cast, though, forged an appropriate style of playing and performed with panache. The words were punchy and witty, as were the songs which came in from time to time. The actors aimed to be jeer-proof and, though there was inappropriate laughter and the odd snide comment, they kept the lid on for most of the time. Nevertheless the emotional orientation of the play invited the audience to lament for the plight of 'poor old us'. The ending may have been a bit negative but at least it provided no glib answer to the besetting problems. There was a whole workshop to come for the airing of those.

The experience of the unemployed was much more coherently and disturbingly protrayed than in *Better in the Long Run* or *Gaining Ground* in the late 1980s by the group from Dublin, Wet Paint. The play, *Dead Ahead*, devised and directed by David Byrne, made no attempt at realism of setting or of style. It focused on a young man being badgered and thwarted on all sides by deliberately caricatured family and officials but himself being abrasive, rebellious and tactless. What gave the piece its edge was the kind of humour it generated, which showed up absurdities in both protagonist and system. The temptation to lurch into pathos was sternly resisted, although the actor playing the young man (Larry Lowry) earned the audience's sympathy by his own obviously genuine sense of the underlying tragedy.

Raj

Raj, created by the Leeds TIE team and writer Paul Swift, raises important issues but does so in an exotic setting, British India during World War Two. In contrast to the two plays we have just been discussing, it achieved national acclaim, was subsequently performed by other companies and was published by Amber Lane Press. In further contrast, *Raj* was a play making its statement in terms of a dramatic artefact alone and not dependent for its educative effect on a follow-up workshop.

Of recent years, the Raj has been a popular subject for dramatic treatment among adults too, with films like *Gandhi*, television series such as *The Jewel in the Crown* and novels like Salman Rushdie's *Midnight Children*. But the Leeds team also had local circumstances in mind, since it worked in an area with a substantial Indian and Pakistani population. The play is not specifically about racialism – it is about imperialism and power, friendship and divided loyalties. Although it deals with concerns that make it of interest to adults, it was targeted at the ten- to twelve-year age range in the first place with some performances, in the event, given to older children too. Paul Swift, the writer, declared his aim in an interview with Geoff Gillham in the *SCYPT Journal*

> to create a play that would actually challenge their preconceptions about their view of the world and of the sort of relationships between white and black people; to engage the kids in subjective responses with the consciousness of broader implications, but that the subjective responses should be something that pulled against the establishment view of the world which they've been fed and which they're imbibing.[4]

What *Raj* strove desperately to do was to avoid polarising the mixed audiences. It wanted the audience to experience detachment from characters both of their own and of another 'race', to enjoy that autonomy which is the goal of both good theatre and education through theatre. It also strove to achieve a balance between public and private experience and it was its spectacular success in doing this that made it deservedly a landmark in the history of theatre for the young in Britain. The play was made accessible to the children in terms of their own familiar experience and it built on that to challenge the mind with wider concerns. 'The major relationships in the play are between parents or surrogate parents and children and between friends; both are strong influences in the lives of 10 to 12 year olds.'[5] It aimed to tell the truth, however disconcerting that might prove. The exotic setting helped to create critical distancing and estrangement.

> The audience's attitudes to authority tended to be such that there seemed little doubt in their minds that Ma-bap (the white mem-sahib) would sort out the problem and provide them with a happy ending. It was through these very personal concerns that the younger age group became involved in considering the complex social and political issues in the play.[6]

Briefly, the story of the play is as follows. The focus is a young Indian woman, Nandita, from her early childhood in the household of a Chief Justice, where she is brought up, through her arranged marriage and early bereavement to her getting a place in the household of Colonel Gower as a nursemaid to his children, James and Elizabeth. She gains this position through her uncle, Ganesh, who is head bearer in the Gower household. Eventually Nandita progresses to become a close friend and confidante of Victoria, the wife of Colonel Gower. Ganesh has a son, Tarun, who enlists, with his father's blessing, in the British Indian Army for the Burmese campaign against the Japanese. Sickened by the way the British behave towards the villagers, Tarun deserts and returns to his father, who hides him. In doing this Ganesh is pulled two ways: he loves his son but he is deeply loyal to the British Raj and to the Gowers. Nandita appeals to Vicky, who tries to help but fails. Tarun is shot seeking to escape when he is discovered hiding in Ganesh's quarters. Ganesh is put on trial for harbouring a deserter, and Nandita makes another appeal, this time to her early guardian, the Chief Justice, but he cannot further any interests that clash with his duty to the Empire. Nandita acknowledges a severance from her British friends.

Leeds TIE team was founded in 1971 and it has encouraged long-stay commitments among the actors. Annalyn Bhanji, an Indian actress born in this country, was a founder member. Certainly a small and compact cast benefited here from familiarity and trust. All the parts were played by one white man, one white woman, one black man and one black woman. Some of the scenes, especially among the coloured actors, cost considerable effort both to create and perform. Paul Swift told me that all efforts to improvise a scene in which Wyllie Longmore, the male coloured actor, as an obstreperous stall-holder refuses to sell a sari to Vicky failed and the scene had to be written for them. When the play was presented to older children, the cast came up against entrenched racial attitudes. What they sensed coming from the white section of the audience was a desire to see Tarun and Ganesh humiliated. This apparently made white actor Mike Kenny play up the authoritarianism of Colonel Gower as against the less blameworthy paternalism. For Wyllie, it meant coming to grips with the terms in which he felt he could allow the characters he played to be debased – a voyage of discovery for him as well as for the audience. Swift described what happened as a temporary loss of faith in the script, but the script was firm enough to re-establish itself. Annalyn experienced a mixed reception with older children as narrator and mediator. No attempt was made to cast white actors as black characters or vice versa. It was felt that the play needed clarity of outline and that something was to be gained by seeing white 'children' inheriting so unthinkingly their father's behaviour and attitudes and black 'children' becoming resentful of the inherited roles.

The style of presentation was open and Brechtian, with no theatrical mysteries hidden from the audience. Sound effects were seen being produced, sometimes by percussion instruments but, more excitingly, by the voices of people on or off stage. The play worked particularly well on the chosen traverse stage. Structurally it consisted of a series of short scenes weaving the story into a background of political and public (sometimes violent) events. In the *SCYPT Journal* interview already referred to, Geoff Gillham elicited comments on the importance of images as well as words and certainly there were self-conscious attempts to show actions in different contexts. Whether they fulfilled the function of embodying 'gesti' of major significance will be open for discussion, when we consider the play in performance in detail.

The performance of 'Raj' at Corpus Christi School, Leeds, by Leeds TIE Company, 27 January 1983

The policy of the company was to play *Raj* to audiences consisting of one class with a maximum of forty pupils. It was with older children (mid teens) that I saw the play. The setting was a big, echoing hall with unscheduled off-stage bangs, voices and shuffling of feet. Despite the loss of intimacy and the threat of distraction, the company played with great commitment and the audience, mostly white, were quiet and attentive. The actors sat on chairs at the four corners of the acting space, and at one end was an all-purpose structure representing a building and made from canvas panels and bamboos.

Nandita introduced the story and we flashed back to a seaside holiday scene between Nandita and her guardian, Chief Justice Courtney Wickham. A note of harmonious affection was struck – very relaxed. The justice gave a locket to Nandita for a Christmas present. Her marriage and widowhood were narrated and we moved into the scene where, briefed by Ganesh, she was interviewed for the job with the Gowers. Ganesh warned her to be respectful: 'You are an Indian peasant and you must show respect.' But, in the event, in spite of her being a bit forward, she secured the appointment. Her vitality burst through the mask, and prepared us for a display of spirit later.

We were shown a scene where the Gowers' children and Tarun play games. Friendly intimacy was established, with an undercurrent of unease on the part of the audience. Tarun played soldiers with young James, and James insisted that Tarun, representing the enemy, must be defeated. Tarun allowed himself to be shot and he fell spreadeagled on the the ground, a position he was to assume again when, towards the end of the play, he was shot in actuality. James next wanted to play 'daddies' and get Tarun, as Ganesh, to clean his shoes. 'Ganesh' refused and this became a 'kneeling' scene that did not come off for the whites. Although only in game, it raised speculation, and established and made use of the character of Tarun. Nandita, talking to Tarun, said: 'I don't see why you want to change things', showing a naïvety from which the audience was invited to distance itself. An all-knowing Nandita would have loosed some crude propaganda and been insufferable.

On the eve of the departure of the regiment, a party was

thrown. The children's dog intruded (made present solely by an actor's voice and the movements of those assembled). It raised alarm as it was thought to be rabid, but was actually plastered with shaving soap by the kids prior to an attempt of shave it. Colonel Gower went over the top, was furious and threatened Ganesh with dismissal for laxity. His authoritarianism was later explained away by his wife as a manifestation of stress, rather than the action of a wicked imperialist. All the same, there was, I felt, a suggestion of overkill in the situation. Although the Colonel's action was explained away, it left a nasty taste. But when he said, quietly, 'There's going to be trouble', he nicely understated the seriousness of the Indian rebellion – a restrained and sensitive performance by Mike Kenny. Colonel Gower was part of the system, too, we felt, trapped by his role into acting occasionally against his nature.

There followed the famous bazaar scene, where Vicky was taken by Nandita to a native shop and attempted to buy a sari. Not only did the furious stall-holder refuse to sell it to her, but he threw it on the floor. Wyllie's shopkeeper was vehement, but, although it was older than the play was originally designed for, this was not a threatening audience and his anger remained within acceptable artistic bounds. The narrator told us of the Indian Congress being dissolved by the British and saw 'trouble' in the town square. This scene came opportunely after the stall-holder incident which had showed us tensions on an individual and personal level. A British soldier shot a protester before Nandita's eyes and this registered as a significant moment for her. But he did it not with sadistic relish but as an unquestioned duty. At the Gower house the rebels killed the dog, Binkie, and in their search for a reason the children were led into considering political matters. Next, the children were bundled off abroad for safety but Vicky still kept Nandita on. There was a genuine mutual fondness on all sides.

Vicky and Nandita found themselves unable to get home because Amritsar station had been destroyed. They were rescued by the British private, Whitely. The irony of his comment: 'Thank goodness for the British army, eh, mum?' might have been a little heavy for adults but for these youngsters the emphasis was about right. News from the Burmese front recorded that Colonel Gower was missing, believed killed. His wife reacted with believable British phlegm. Ganesh's son, Tarun, was also missing, but Ganesh suffered the torments of the guilty.

Then Tarun turned up, a deserter! He was allowed a long, exonerating speech which justified his anger at the British. Nandita complicated the audience response by saying: 'You talk about the British as if they were all the same', and this, her personal view, was understandable in the context of the play.

Nandita told us that Tarun was now holed up with Ganesh, and we saw Ganesh in a nervous state being goaded by Vicky, who was also overwrought. She demanded tea and he dropped the tray. The teacup ended up in three pieces. According to the published volume, a child in the audience at another performance found the fact that the cup did this highly significant. It was, the child said, 'like India' which itself ended up in three pieces. The right to a personal reaction has to be conceded, of course, but I doubt it was obvious to many people. What was made obvious was the battle of wills as Ganesh hesitated before he could bring himself to pick up the pieces as ordered. A huge pause was held, far longer than was necessary here, even with an audience like this. Would not it have been perfectly reasonable for Ganesh to pick up something he had dropped? Could it really carry the particular significance with which it was loaded? Nandita told Vicky, afterwards, the real reason for Ganesh's nervousness and the Mem-sahib promised to help. She did so by making a phone call to the Brigadier. But it was not clear what she would say. Would she, out of character, actually betray the boy? Was the vagueness at this point a cop-out or a successful dramatic ambiguity? Anyway, Tarun was shot leaving Ganesh's quarters and the two women looked at each other, expressionless, over the dead body. Nandita told us of Ganesh's arrest and imprisonment. She left Vicky's employment of her own accord and, significantly, refrained (for ever) from opening the farewell present that Vicky gave her.

Nandita made a petition on her knees to the Chief Justice for his help in mitigating Ganesh's sentence, but Wickham preferred his duty to King and Country. Nandita, snubbed, returned the locket to him. A nicely rounded and downbeat ending.

To sum up: I came away from the performance of *Raj* thinking I had witnessed a good production of one of the best plays aimed at children that I had ever seen. It judged the comprehension level very accurately and led the audience to an awareness of the larger social and political context in which the accessible personal interactions were set. *Raj* raised issues but managed to achieve the dramatic balance that John Arden so prizes.[7] The actors themselves had strong feelings about the subject but, as Wyllie Longmore points out, 'You must pull back from that, and let the play go through its natural course to get at those racist ideas, rather than to use it as a bludgeoning instrument.'[8] Just occasionally I sensed in the performance a little self-conscious portentousness. The interviews in the *SCYPT Journal* make a lot of the use of significant images, particularly the image of kneeling. But the writing was complex and the impact more subtle than a detachment of images might suggest. The Brits being knelt to, or demanding to be knelt to, were shown in a sympathetic light as well as a critical one. The acting was restrained and it showed that plays for children do not need to be strident in their presentation or obviously 'out front'. The ending, with help for Nandita refused by Wickham, was dramatically right and logical.

The theme of cultural identity and the need for mutual respect across the cultures was to become very popular later in the 1980s. In *Lilford Mill* by Pitprop from Leigh in Lancashire, the question is posed why German prisoners in World War One were transferred from Ireland to mainland Britain. Could it be that the Irish and the Germans had common cause against the 'enemy', the British? This play, too, scores by concentrating on turning two German prisoners and two girls into interesting and credible individuals. On a political level, though, it was a little starry-eyed about the IRA and, unlike *Raj*, presented the British simplistically as inept and insensitive.

Half Moon's hour-long piece for upper juniors, *Dear Suraiya . . . Love Rehana*, was a problem play about the sufferings of the tea-planters in Bangladesh whose water supply is not fit to drink. The story unfolds through the correspondence between the two cousins named in the title, one living in England, where tea is drunk, and the other where tea is grown. A challenge is presented to the Chairman of the tea compnay when a glass of water arrives in England for him to set an example by drinking. Will he, won't he? So that the play itself will be a multi-cultural event, there are commentaries and dialogue in both English and Sylheti, reflecting the real-life experiences of the communities of Tower Hamlets in London and treating the two languages as equally important. A clever idea, but the play had its eye too firmly fixed on the follow-up work to make much *dramatic* impact.

The Plays of David Holman

David Holman has as big a name to be conjured with in the sphere of issue-based politically conscious plays as David Wood has in his. His works include *Rare Earth, The Disappeared, Inuit, No Pasaran, 1983, ABC* and *Gawwaine and the Green Knight*. *Susumu's Story* and *Peacemaker* we have already mentioned. The choice of an exotic setting is one of his hallmarks. In 1981, he declared himself less interested in 'messages' than in widening children's horizons (literally).

> I think I used to be a bit more messianic about imposing what I believed on other people. . . . And probably it is a realisation that my own particular views or artistic interests or whatever are quite individual and not something laid down or recommended to other people. What I am interested in now is in a sense bringing the far away – that could well be in historical or geographical terms – into the lives of the children. That I find is basically what I like to do.[9]

At his best, though, the concern of a committed person comes through in his writing. Through experiencing other people's cultures and observing both the similarities with and differences from their own, the audience find a way of looking at themselves also.

I have seen two of his plays in a school, *Susumu's Story* and *Peacemaker*, one that had been in schools and was enjoying a performance in Nottingham Playhouse itself

(*No Pasaran*) and one which was shown to delegates at a SCYPT conference (*ABC*).

The setting for *Susumu's Story* is Hiroshima in Japan during World War Two. The play is for Juniors (about nine years old) and is an example of the forty-five-minute piece. This is a very difficult form to handle if the writer/deviser has ambitions to produce more than a simple story. David Holman tries to provide a focal situation with which an audience can connect and to suggest the larger public context which will enable him to make some sort of statement about the desirability of peace. He does not choose the 'programme' form, that is to say he tries to make his meanings in terms of the completed artefact. As he says in the *SCYPT Journal* 'I think the best 45 minute shows are closed, in that they must have an ending which implies a sort of totality. But it must also buzz off back to particular areas, it must also leave question marks.'[10]

The story: Susumu, a young Japanese boy, is the narrator and the channel for messages. Here, Holman chooses a strategy he discarded when writing *No Pasaran*, that of seeing the action through the eyes of the erstwhile enemy, in the case of *No Pasaran* seeing the Jew through German eyes. Susumu declares that he is telling the story of Kiyoko, a girl friend, and that it will range over the period covered by four of her birthdays, starting with the eleventh, the 'year Japan went to war'. The initial Japanese military triumphs are enacted for us by two Kabuki figures, sparring in the background. Susumu gives Kiyoko a present of a dragonfly in a matchbox but she is sad that it has unnecessarily died. He then gives her a cherry blossom which he has stolen from the park, but she insists he takes it back. Kiyoko's mother, Mrs Ogimura, tells the children the cat has pulled father's uniform off the clothes line and the chickens have decorated it. The kids try not to laugh aloud. Susumu is enthusiastic about the war and he indulges in Walter Mitty fantasies about being a pilot. But he is too young and has only one hair in his 'beard'. Like *Raj*, the play uses war-games to highlight childish misconceptions. Mrs Ogimura has knitted a scarf for her husband and will present it to him before he sets off for the war. The fathers do leave and Susumu reflects that although he did not cry then, he would have done if he had known what was going to happen in the future. The Kabuki USA bullies a magician (scientist!) into making a super-bomb. Kiyoko's thirteenth birthday finds the kids in school playing with gas-masks. Susumu, immature as ever, has swallowed the official optimistic propaganda and is rebuked by the wise Kiyoko: 'Always the tatatatata. It's not a game. What's going on in your head when they read out all those names in school? The boys and girls that used to be at this school that are dead already. Burnt in planes, drowned at sea.' The teacher, Mr Hagawa, has lost his own son and this makes Susumu look very tactless when he mouths the 'Dulce et decorum est' platitudes. Hagawa proposes they help the war effort by digging up the playground and planting vegetables and trees. Kiyoko wants to plant a tree. The USA, meanwhile, tests a bomb. For her fourteenth birthday, Kiyoko expects the return of her father. With her usual perspicacity, she knows that Japan is losing the war. Susumu's family are retreating to the country for safety – in case Hiroshima is bombed. Kiyoko is attending to her tree when the atom bomb arrives. Susumu delivers a short oration, enjoining the audience to do something about these weapons.

The performance of 'Susumu's Story' at Sandiway County Primary School, Cheshire, by Theatre Centre, 21 September 1982

The play was presented in the round to a well-controlled audience of upper juniors. They were able to see and were interested in the changes of costume and character and the making of sound-effects. The choice of Susumu as narrator meant that the kids had both to go along with him and, at times, distance themselves from him. They related to the scenes where children were being children and laughed heartily: scenes such as when Susumu boasts of his one facial hair and where the chickens dirty the uniform. He had, rather heavily, to point out the coming menace of which the innocent Japanese children were unaware. A refined version of the 'Look, he's behind you!' routine perhaps? Some actual audience participation was invited by the cast and of a surprisingly 'directed' kind. One actress tried to get the audience clapping the Japanese victory but signally failed. Whether the kids remembered that the Japanese had been the enemy or whether they were overawed by the occasion I do not know. They also refused to sing 'Happy Birthday to Kiyoko'. They were promised a go at digging up the playground but it never came.

Despite Susumu's best efforts, I did wonder how far this young audience made the necessary connections. The personal story had to be left from time to time so that the political and military background could be enacted and commented upon. The USA looked truly villainous, but he and his Japanese counterpart were supposed to represent something we could all grow into. I wondered how far they could connect the childish war-games of the kids in the play with such dire consequences, or whether the USA was just, to them, the traditional baddie figure, absolute evil coming from outside (like David Wood's oil slick?) or a natural disaster. Were the audience helped to understand the springs of violence? I had my doubts. Much of the forty-five minutes being diverted from the main story meant that the main story was rather thin and that Holman did not have the elbow-room to create characters whose fate one could care enough about to be galvanised into endorsement of the 'peace' message. One curious fact – when it was all over, there was no applause and the kids were decidedly restless after the second explosion

The other play in the Holman duo which I have referred to earlier in connection with the issue of censorship is *Peacemaker*. The story of this is as follows: we are invited by a narrator to 'come with us into the land of red, where our story begins'. The table concerns the red people and the blue people who 'come and go, go and come' as they please at first, over the bridge that joins their two countries, in a spirit of co-operation and friendliness. But one day a wall is erected separating them. A red girl practises juggling for a carnival but she is not good at it. The ruler of the reds comes on and tells stories of the monsters that live on the other side of the wall. One day when the red girl is juggling, one of her balls goes over and a blue man appears over the wall. He protests that the rumours are wrong about blues killing people and he is relieved to learn that the reds do not either. The blue man would like to demonstrate the art of dancing but the wall prevents this. A gap in the wall is created and the blue man comes over. The red boss returns, forcing the reds to hide the blue boy by sitting on him. The boss orders the wall to be rebuilt but the underlings secretly punch a hole in it and the mutual signalling continues.

The performance of 'Peacemaker' at Sandiway County Primary School, Cheshire, by Theatre Centre, 21 September 1982

I saw this play the same day as I saw *Susumu's Story* and in the same place. This time the audience were infants. The cast consisted of two male and two female actors, two black and two white. *Peacemaker* seemed to succeed well on that occasion as an absorbing piece of theatre, well suited to the chosen age group. The audience sat in a horseshoe, with teachers looming behind. At the open end of the horseshoe was a large wall, draped in blue and red sheets. This served as the bridge between the two countries and friendly encounters were enacted by means of puppets. Later it transformed itself – to a gasp from the audience – into a wall, as the coverings were removed. There was other theatrical magic (though not of the illusionary David Wood kind) when a blue-green sheet was shaken into ripples to represent the sea and a yellow sheet spread to represent the desert.

Holman himself professes to be a devotee of emotional impact in theatre for the young. In *Susumu's Story*, the atomic explosions were frightening; in *Peacemaker*, it was the appearance of a hand belonging to a black actor playing a 'blue' on the top of the wall that set one small girl crying. A teacher rushed to comfort her. When a gap was forced in the wall and this large black 'blue' came striding through it to the accompaniment of noisy percussion it was the turn of a small boy to be shocked into tears. Joyce McMillan, reviewing the performance of *Peacemaker* by Theatre About Glasgow, referred to earlier, found the noise excessive. 'Director Maggie Kinlock has gone too hard for pace and impact in the production, producing a lot of loud bangs, shrillness and confusion and frightening some of the younger kids half to death'.[11] For fear to be susceptible to catharsis one could argue, it needs to be experienced. This fear was built into the story and was not gratuitous. Perhaps there was some risk in casting a black man as an imagined 'monster' of implanting that negro image in the mind. But the actor not only made the most of his warm encounters with the reds and of the hiding-from-the-boss routine to rouse sympathetic laughter, but stepped out of role before their very eyes, later, to chat to the audience and to make a special effort to befriend the two weepers. I think on the whole the play contained the necessary reassurance in itself, though. The ending was legitimately hopeful. The acting was on the whole appropriate to the presentation, being vigorous and insisting on showing as well as telling. In its efforts to grab the attention, it was a trifle noisy and it should be remembered that kids can take some quiet acting too. There was some obligatory audience participation of the peripheral kind, with the same object in view.

At the end, the audience were asked to decide for themselves what could happen to the wall now. Joyce McMillan voted the response to this the saving grace: 'The quirky originality of the children's ideas salvages the play from trendy-lefty twee-ness.'[12]

With *ABC*, Theatre Centre and David Holman again put their dramatic powers at the service of a cause, this time the Literacy Crusade in Nicaragua.

> The Literacy Crusade was launched in 1980. Under Somoza, the illiteracy rate was 54% in urban areas and 80% in rural areas – in the most remote regions, it was reaching 100% illiteracy. Illiteracy in Nicaragua is now down to 12% The work of the Crusade was mainly carried out by young volunteers; over 60,000 young people went in teams to the country areas to teach reading and writing. (Information sheet distributed by Theatre Centre)

ABC is really about the power of words, although the political applications of such power are strongly implied. It focuses on a peasant family – Violetta, the mother, her daughters Mercedes and Rosa – and on the new teacher, Lea. We meet the family as they are preparing for a festival and want words for their respective banners. It is a matter of finding the most appropriate ones in each case. A series of narrations introduces episodes illustrating significant events in their lives. Violetta tells how her daughter was killed by one of the General's guards and how she pleaded for the girl's life. The most attractive concept for her is FREEDOM. The killer of the child is nicknamed the 'dog'. Mercedes tells how the Dog was captured by Sandinista guerrillas, how Violetta was given the option of 'revenge' or 'justice' and how she chose justice. JUSTICE is Mercedes's banner slogan. Rosa's word is illustrated by the story of how she was given a consignment of parrots to deliver to the USA. She is stopped by patriots and the parrots are released. Some die but others will survive, we are told. Rosa's word becomes PARROT.

In the discussion that followed – at the 1983 SCYPT Conference – some of the delegates were unhappy about the 'justice' scene. The writer and the company were accused of 'papering over the class nature of justice' and of endorsing the impartiality of state justice (a sell-out to the bourgeois?). Surely peasant justice demanded that the Dog be summarily executed? I wondered myself if the only notion of justice that an audience of youngsters might come away with might be that justice meant not killing the accused. Other people must have had similar unease as there were questions about what subsequently is supposed to have happened to the Dog. Could somebody else have shot him?

There were references to the help given to the peasants by Oxfam and Christian Aid, and some delegates, again, took the play to task for not spelling out explicitly that gifts from these organisations represented a sop thrown to the peasants by the imperialists, and for hiding the real involvement of Great Britain with the former Nicaraguan ruling class and with President Reagan. People also thought that the liberating power of education ought to have been put over more starkly.

Many of these objections to the play were to what people saw as ideological misrepresentation. But surely it is *artistic* truth we are demanding – or ought to be. An overloading of messages can defeat both propagandist and artistic aims when the autonomy of artists and audience are ignored.

> It's one of the worst faults of TIE or children's theatre and maybe of social political theatre in general. The worst thing you can do is to have a pint pot but insist to the audience that they are going to get a quart's worth. That leads to a particular form of strangulated theatre where for every half page of script, you are getting a page of footnotes.[13]

Holman said he was trying to back off from psychological bullying, and the objections of the politically minded critics would seem to indicate that he was succeeding. There was some successful particularising in the play. 'Parrots', although heavily symbolic, has the virtue of concreteness, especially for children. Its incongruity gave rise to laughter even at the SCYPT Conference, and its choice was appropriate to the *character* of Rosa as developed in the play, where she is shown as naïve, headstrong and lazy. Her mother's sufferings at the death of her other daughter were movingly evoked. The all-female cast of four played all the parts – including the General's guard and the Dog. We were told that one aim of the company was to create 'positive images' of women, and it is true that by implication an extra fillip was given to the plea for 'rights'.

No Pasaran pre-dates *ABC* and the other 'peace' plays in Holman's output, being first performed in January 1977 at Bolton Theatre Studio. It is the more overtly propagandist play that Holman says he is subsequently concerned to tone down. It was published by Methuen.

No Pasaran is the story of a Jewish boxer who wants to take part in the 1936 Olympics as a German entrant but is stopped because he is a Jew. He goes to England with two British athletes and takes part in the Cable Street battle with Mosley's Fascists. He returns to Germany for his parents and disappears.

The performance of 'No Pasaran' at the Nottingham Playhouse by the Roundabout TIE Company, 28 September 1983

On this occasion, *No Pasaran* played to an almost full house (capacity 500) of fifth-year students. The event was part of a Peace Studies experiment of which the first part was a performance of *O What a Lovely War*, performed in schools. The third part was to follow in the new year. A working party in Nottingham produced the County Council Peace Report, whose remit was to look into the problems of introducing peace studies in schools. The production of *No Pasaran* benefited from an access of money from the Labour-controlled local authorities. The schools had to be persuaded to give up three whole days for all the fifth-year pupils and not just the 'less able'.

Before the performance that I saw, which began at 1.30 p.m., there had been a morning workshop consisting of slides, a film about Hitler's rise and a discussion with actors in the theatre.

Rick Hall, the Director of the company, said this particular performance was adapted from a film/television version of the play and not simply the printed text. It started and ended with Sammy McEvoy, the British friend of Goldberg, attempting to trace the Jewish boy after the war. Stirring Nazi music, loud and exciting, conveyed the exhilaration that German youth must have experienced when Nazism was on the rise. There were classroom scenes (helping the audience to identify?) which introduced the hero, Jan Goldberg, and his aspirations to box for Germany in the Olympics. Hitler Youth propagandists got at the pupils inside and outside the school. In the school, a formal debate was set up between the converted Nazi boy and Jan. This showed the case the Nazis were making out without showing how the attitude developed.

The story of Goldberg was supposed to personalise and unify the action, but there was a heavy concentration on background events and the thread at times got lost. We had debates between the teacher, Mrs Schmidt, and a party official, and between her and her husband, she being the voice of reason. Slides were projected of the public events with varying effect. In the protective darkness of the auditorium, some of the youngsters giggled at the pictures of the skeletal victims of Dachau concentration camp. The narrators were more effective at grabbing their attention (for example at the end of the play where a woman survivor tells of the process of gassing).

The English boxers who befriended Jan introduced a note of good-humoured sanity and light-heartedness. There was good scene where they tricked the prejudiced waiter in a café into serving the young Jew. Here, a handy radio broadcast the news from the Olympics of Jesse Owen's triumphs (he being an American negro). This is, of course, very relevant to the story of Jan who is deprived of his Olympic outlet. Jan offered to be a sparring partner for Sammy. Tactlessly asked why he was not an official German contender, he angrily laid into the British boy, thereby expressing subconsciously his desire for violent revenge on behalf of all Jewish victims and fulfilling the audience's wishes, too. At this point it came to seem slightly odd to have our fighter wreaking violent vengeance in a 'peace' play. But still . . .

An attempt was made to link up the historical experience with the familiar lives of the young spectators. A timely comparison between Nazi rallies and a football crowd was apposite. There was an implicit comparison between the Nazis and our National Front of today, and one of the causes of Fascism, the fact of there being six million unemployed in Germany, must have reverberated in the minds of the particular generation watching the play.

The second half was more bitty. 'Rule Britannia' led us in, intended, I imagine, to be ironic, but the youngsters sang along with it. Jan soon met the British equivalent of the German brownshirts and was beaten up. A gratuitous appeal to the audience 'Why didn't you stop it?' seemed unfair and clumsy. The youngsters did, spontaneously, clap at the defeat of the British Fascist marchers in Cable Street. The ending of the play restrained itself from tying up the ends too neatly and the woman who told us all about the death camps did not, after all, know Jan Goldberg.

As a play, the personal story got swamped by the historical background. There was a lot of wordy debate and narration, and some conclusions were explicitly encouraged. We did not have enough insight into what causes individuals to embrace or reject Fascism. There was a sufficiency of emotional impact, though, enhanced by the darkened auditorium. The setting was striking, not to say lurid, with huge banner swastikas. Possibly some of the deficiencies were made good in the accompanying workshops, but the play was also written as a self-sufficient unit – 'closed', in Holman's own word – and qualified to be judged in those terms.

Refugee, by Frances McNeil, was also part of the Nottingham Roundabout Company's contribution to Peace Studies. It, too, took the form of a complete play and was embedded in a whole-day programme as the 'key' experience.

The story: *Refugee* was an episodic study of people made homeless by forces outside their control. They are victims of political events. The main character is a girl, Binh Chao, who is a Chinese living in Vietnam, near Hanoi. She learns in school about the history of the country. At one point she proves herself to be a good Vietnamese by giving away the whereabouts of a hidden. American soldier. When the American bombing becomes too close for comfort, she is evacuated with her family to grandmother's place in the country. But she has to flee again from there to Hong Kong, in company with a Mr Mann whom she dislikes. She actually lands first in China after the boat is wrecked and she is forced to work in a commune. Mann is a capitalist by inclination and he wants to go to America. They escape and manage to reach Hong Kong where they are housed in a refugee camp. Refugees are subjected to the blandishments of the representatives of the USA, Sweden, Australia and Britain. She is directed to go to Britain. Eventually, on learning to speak English, she starts to drift away from the Vietnamese community.

I saw the play performed at the Regional Conference of SCYPT in Nottingham in February 1983, and the delegates (about thirty, and all in TIE) discussed it afterwards. I found the play too generalised. There were altogether too many issues, too much information banged at the audience. There was widespread agreement that the play attempted too much, took too wide a sweep. It was David Holman's pint pot attempting to accommodate a quart all over again. One actor felt that the play needed a stronger focus on the character of the girl as there was little real interest in her as a person. Her relationship with her parents was not built up sufficiently for us to be concerned about what happened to them. It was felt that there was a potentially interesting personal conflict with the man in the boat which was a lost opportunity.

There might, though, have been difficulties in fulfilling the aims of the programme if the play had focused too narrowly on the girl. They could not show the girl as being particularly sophisticated in politics as it would then not have been so easy to raise the range of issues with the audience. Rick Hall, the director, thought that this was a basic problem of the format – a performance of a play followed by role-play and discussion. The writer must have an eye on the potential for follow-up work.

In the 'workshop' session, the actors – in role – answer questions from the kids, about the girl's life in Vietnam, for instance. They ask the kids to pretend they have been kicked out of Britain and have to decide what they will take with them, where they will go and what they feel like to be homeless. A woman in the company said the actors got too involved and there just was not time to reassure the kids. There could be a case, then, for relying more on the play to do the 'distancing' for them.

In the afternoon of the conference, there was a revealing discussion about the educational and artistic motives of the performers, ostensibly to deal with the subject of treating peace studies through TIE. One young woman objected to the whole business of peace studies as a subject. Anyway, how did this play contribute to peace studies? As *No Pasaran* did – I suppose – by showing conflicts. But another faction made no bones about stating that 'our' business as TIE workers was to convey a left-wing message. An objection was raised to messages and loaded dice and a plea for greater subtlety in the plays was made. Some agreed that this meant the objector simply wanted the message disguised. Reference was made to John Arden's appeal for artistic balance and we were warned that if writers and devisers followed that theory through, the kids might sympathise with the capitalists, which would never do. But, as has been observed, crude propaganda can be counter-productive. One woman wondered what action their work might lead the kids to embark upon, given they were too young actually to vote. But surely there is an educative impact in the experience of a good play, anyway, leading to enlightenment and a change of attitude and sympathy.

7

'Social Realism' and Plays Based on other Issues

We now come to a set of plays that raise social and moral issues without being overtly or predominantly political. These, too, operate within the logic of the known and the recognisable. This is true even when the setting is exotic and the action removed from the everyday behaviour of modern children, as is the case with a number of adaptations of children's books, such as *The Railway Children, The Secret Garden, Cider with Rosie* and *Treasure Island*. *Treasure Island* has already been referred to in connection with *Peter Pan*, where Stevenson's full-blooded pirates were put to the service of harmless fantasy. *Treasure Island* does not set out to explore moral issues but the potential for such a venture is there in the book. It is up to the adaptor either to take up the challenge or settle for cashing in on a good, romantic story.

The performance of 'Treasure Island' by the Sheffield Crucible Company at the Crucible Theatre, Sheffield, 16 December 1983

This was a Christmas show aimed at 'the family' or rather

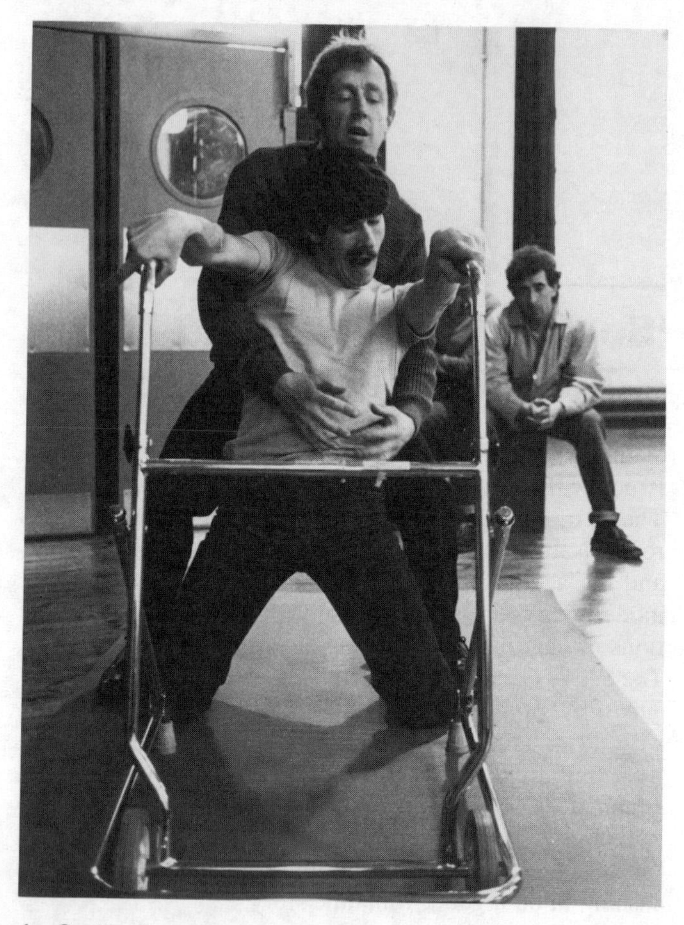

4. *On His Own Two Feet* by Chris Hawes (photograph © Gerry Murray).

at somewhere between the adults and the children. Unfortunately it ended up being completely satisfying to neither section of the audience.

There were, of course, difficulties for the adaptor, Euan Smith. The book is narrated by the main character, Jim Hawkins, and it is easier for the book to direct our attention to his personal development and his changing moral stance. The book more easily copes with changes of location and with the nature of the action. The story is that of a hunt on the part of Captain Smollett, Squire Trelawney, Dr Livesey and Jim himself, on the one hand, and Silver (who was travelling with this party as ship's cook) and a ruffianly crew, on the other, for treasure buried on an island. The pirates reveal themselves for what they are and mutiny. Throughout the story there is a special relationship between Jim Hawkins and Silver. Silver is not above playing both ends against the middle. His sheer audacity takes Jim's breath away and Jim finds conventional moral categories impossible to apply to him. In this stage version, this central relationship lacked subtlety and complexity while the storyline was not stark or emphatic enough to hold the restless young in the audience.

Emotional reactions were skated over in the preoccupation with 'adventure'. Jim and his mother were reconciled in a matter of seconds to the loss of their home. You had to be quick to realise that Jim had got into the apple-barrel at all, let alone that he was reacting to the revelations with horror. What won applause were the swash-buckling action scenes with their deafening gunfire and the ingenuity of the stage-effects. Michael Boyd, the director, made spectacular use of the Crucible's splendid machinery as the ship revolved and the Benbow collapsed in flames. Unfortunately narrative carried by a song which covered the scene changes competed with them for attention and the most successful use of musical accompaniment was in the shanties and work-songs. The setting, in 'thrust', had a shelf running round its rim, while the centre was structured variously as an island or a well, but this area dominated and important developments were sometimes relegated to the shelf. Interesting use was made of sepulchral gloom; it was out of this that a tapping heralded the approach of the sinister Blind Pew.

There was some self-conscious attempt to develop themes; for instance, that of 'trust', and there was some play with the name of 'Silver' as it was here Flint's silver (not his gold) that everybody was after. The effect of this was to simplify Long John. He was more purely the self-seeking villain, albeit the actor, Philip Whitchurch, brought out his smoothness and his sardonic humour well. Silver's precise relationship with Jim, almost that of father and son, was never fully explored. At the beginning of the play, though, we did see the appearance of Jim's real father! Silver's fondness for Jim was not really evident. Jim was useful to him, rather. The pirates in this stage version did approach the condition of Captain Hook's. They did not seem enough of a threat to Silver and Silver never seemed terribly discomfited by them when they rebelled. He was altogether too much in control of things.

Another writer, Rony Robinson, told me that when he had adapted *Treasure Island* for the professional stage it had been interesting to point up the basic similarity of aim and ambition between the law-abiding and the law-breaking members of the expedition, all dazzled by the prospect of personal wealth. In Euan Smith's version, Trelawney was played 'young' like Jim and having to learn humility. Smollett and Livesey did not impress themselves on the mind as creating any particular significance. Ben Gunn, ex-pirate castaway, got a laugh from the very young, but then so did the death of Billy Bones!

YPT companies have shown a more self-conscious interest in raising social and moral questions and have, by and large, preferred a more modern setting.

Example was a complete play, partly devised, partly written, partly assembled by members of the Coventry Belgrade TIE team and writer, Stephen Wyatt, in the mid 1970s. It was published in the same volume as *No Pasaran*. *Example*, though, was about a real-life crime and trial, that which led to the execution of Derek William Bentley in January 1952, who was the 'example' of the title. Reading books on the subject, the company were seized with a sense of outrage and indignation, and this gave the play the appropriate emotional impact. The danger is that some of this emotion will be a distorted, sentimental pity for Bentley, he being the victim of exploitation and intellectually backward to boot. Talking of polemical theatre, Eric Bentley (the critic) says:

> The aim being to re-create the author's sense of outrage, the method is not to use 'rounded', 'human', equally-right-and-wrong characters but enactors of the outrageous on the one hand and, on the other, victims of outrage and rebels against outrage.[1]

But although the workshop scheduled to follow invited the audience to consider the evidence for themselves, the actual evidence is that of the play itself. Its success as a play is what makes the action credible.

The performance of 'Example' at Garibaldi School, Mansfield, by the Nottingham Roundabout Company, 5 October 1982

Example was presented on a multi-purpose set against recessed screens and before an audience of upper secondary pupils in a raked hall. There was a good deal of history to fill in at the beginning as the context for the main story – possibly more than the audience could connect up. Lord Goddard, the Lord Chief Justice and a ruthless authoritarian, was introduced and kept reappearing as a link figure. The sight of him in his judicial robes drew forth a laugh from this audience.

Eventually the main action started with Bentley in class at school in 1947. The teacher used Peter Nichols's *Joe Egg* technique of addressing the audience as the class, telling off one member and humiliating Bentley in front of them. A good choice of scene, as the classroom bullying was something the audience had experienced and observed in their own lives. The teacher was totally brutal but the dialogue was only too credible.

Next, Bentley got involved in stealing and appeared in a juvenile court. He came over as dim, gullible and – in a non-legal sense – innocent, but the magistrate sent him away to three years of 'corrective training'.

We were introduced to sixteen-year-old Christopher Craig and friend, Norman Parsley, talking about Bentley being released from the institution and about his potential as a partner in crime. Craig was now ready to meet Bentley and the scene between them was well written. Craig played cruelly but with sardonic wit on Bentley's weaknesses and the audience learned just how dangerous Craig was. He described his latest crimes, one of which involved robbing an old woman. He found it highly amusing and when he described how the old lady 'peed herself', the audience joined in the laughter. Was it a lapse of tone in the play or was it a tribute to the charisma of Craig? When Bentley expressed reluctance to take part in any more breaches of the law, Craig blackmailed him. When Parsley, the other boy, stepped out of the scene to become Goddard, it helped enforce the relevance of the episode to what Goddard said about the state of crime in general. Bentley, in all this, was the complete victim, weak but blameless.

Compared with the previous scene, the scene that now ensued between Bentley and his mother was rather flat. She ordered him to stay away from Craig, and she got rid of Craig when he called for her son. Craig threatened her and she alerted the police who said they could not do anything. In an effective sequence of short scenes, Craig proposed another job to Parsley who had been thinking and now had doubts.

CRAIG: You shouldn't do it, son.
PARSLEY: [Frightened] What?
CRAIG: Think.
PARSLEY: Oh yeah. [Weak laugh]

The actor playing Craig bellowed out the 'think', making Parsley and the audience jump a foot in the air: a very effective theatrical tactic, reinforcing the terror Craig embodied. Parsley offered to rope in Bentley if he himself could be let off and Craig agreed. The scene which followed was the crucial one, the one in which the murder occurred. Bentley appeared, dressed in a trilby and raincoat and looking both pathetic and ridiculous. The audience giggled. With Craig, he climbed on to the roof of a warehouse in Croydon, but the police found out and arrived in force. The police attempted to arrest the boys, one policeman (Sergeant Fairfax) was wounded and one (PC Miles) killed. Some details of what happened were disputed (for example whether Bentley was technically under arrest at the time of the shooting by Craig) and since the 'truth' was never known, the play had to be careful not to be too clear. We saw the crime from Craig's point of view first and then in Sergeant Fairfax's account.

> All these things now happen together. Craig aims wildly, Bentley and Fairfax separate. It's not clear whether Bentley had pulled away or not or whether he has said anything. Fairfax falls to the ground and Bentley moves to him. No sound.

The 'framing' of the events within a point of view enabled the writers to show us the scene and remind us how relative the 'facts' were.

In a crude send-up of the Press, a newspaper account was shown. Bentley, in custody, was interviewed by an unsympathetic defence counsel, Cassels. He spelled out to Bentley what a formidable prosecutor Christmas Humphreys was. Giggling greeted almost all the appearances of Bentley but the audience were very attentive once the scenes got under way. In court, Humphreys, played effectively by a woman, made mincemeat of Bentley. Goddard's summing up inexorably stacked the cards against the boy, too.

The death sentence was pronounced and the process began of trying to get it reversed. Tension mounted. The Press were revelling in the drama and appeared in a very critical light in the context. Mrs Bentley struggled heroically but ineffectually. The events were well documented and this lent an air of authority to the material.

Much of the play, though, was fiction posing as fact. The play was intended as a plea for sympathy for Bentley who was convicted of aiding and abetting a murderer on some dicey evidence. It did try to show the pressures that made lawyers and policemen harsh, vindictive and in need of an 'example' to deter others. The giggling of the audience, though, seemed to me to indicate that the performance alienated them from Bentley to a degree not intended. One can never be sure with laughter in the theatre, but it did not sound like an escape valve for embarrassing feelings of compassion. However, the play was, on the whole, a convincing enactment of the crushing of the helpless under the machinery of the system and it left some teasing questions in the mind.

Arthur Rosebud's Revelation, written by two members of the Daylight Theatre Company (consisting of three women and two men), recommends that the members of the audience apply themselves to conserving energy, but does not incite them to change the political system.The play was in fact commissioned by the Department of Energy. It concerns Arthur Rosebud, an eccentric millionaire (modelled, I suspect, on Scrooge) who devotes his time to the invention of labour-saving devices but is unaware that his inventions consume a great deal of power. The arrival of some mysterious visitors eventually makes him see the metaphorical light and he realises the importance of not wasting our natural resources. To the extent that the bulk of the action is dreamed, the play is fantasy but the framework is real life.

The performance of 'Arthur Rosebud's Revelation' in Portland Comprehensive School, Worksop, by Daylight Theatre Company, 18 November 1982

The school hall was full of middle teenagers and they sat on four sides of the acting space in the middle of which was a high, raised platform with an intriguing box on it. It turned out that Arthur Rosebud was in the box and he 'woke up' and delivered a soliloquy over his Scrooge-like hoard of money. His Guardian Angel entered in blue overalls, provoking laughter from the spectators. Then a Robot entered with some zany, over-the-top acting as it went haywire. This, too, was genuinely funny. The appearance of the robot helped, with its eyes on long springs (from a joke shop). Arthur rang up Waldo, a rich American rival who had made his millions with his factories as Arthur had with his inventions. The Energy Efficiency Committee rang Arthur to put its views. The Angel warned Arthur of his impending decease: 'Buckets must be kicked. Final whistles must be blown.' Arthur would be given another chance to get things right in a future reincarnation but he was more concerned to make another million in this life.

His niece came in, wearing green hair and sporting a pink plastic bag and boots. She graced us with a song:

> I don't wanna go to school
> I don't wanna be anybody's fool
> I wanna be free
> I wanna be me.

After this corny anarchic outburst, she suddenly snapped into another mode of address and warned Arthur and the audience that the world's resources of gas and oil were going to run out shortly: 'There's an energy gap and I'm going to fill it.' The sudden assumption of the role of Enlightened Youth did not fit the language and concepts of the defiant punk. The message came out very starkly. Then this actress became someone out of a previous life and talked to Arthur about the inventions they had collaborated on in the past. The girl is a ghost now: 'Let's say I'm just sitting this life out.'

Arthur had promised the Board 'up there' to make the most of his opportunities, but he wasted energy. 'What does it matter when I can afford it?' His house had no thermal insulation. An Energy Inspector with a long joke-shop nose came in and arrested Arthur. 'Your time's running out. You'll be living in the Arctic Circle next life.' A song followed: 'Nothing lasts for ever.'

The play ended with the conversion of Arthur and became a bit too earnest. Arthur declared: 'I shall repair my house at one.' He would get the roof lagged and so on. He gave money to the Robot: 'Use it throughout the world that it may nourish the coming of a new age.' A portentous pronouncement indeed! He had conquered and 'left his world behind him'.

Arthur Rosebud's Revelation was the vehicle for a pre-packaged message and it suffered from it. There was no feeling that it sprang from the deep personal concerns of writers and artists who produced it, or that they grew by exploring it, as happens in the best 'committed' theatre, like *Raj*. This was more like a commercial than a play. The qualities of fantasy were exploited to make possible the baldest of moralising. We did not see the creative anarchy of a Ken Campbell. The tone of the piece was inconsistent, but the acting was consistently strident. The comic talents of the performers, however, were beyond dispute as they won deservedly hearty laughs. At one point, though, I saw youngsters reading books surreptitiously as the performance washed over them. In the follow-up discussion, most of the questions were about the lives and previous careers of the actors, which could say something about the dialectical interest of the play.

Roy Kift and GRIPS

Roy Kift is a writer who introduced the work of the West German Children's Theatre GRIPS into Great Britain. Growing out of cabaret, the GRIPS company acquired its name (equivalent to the idiomatic English word 'nous') in 1972. Kift's own association with them began in 1979. He states their preoccupations as follows: 'GRIPS, quite simply, concerns itself with the everyday problems of children in their relationships with adults and the world around them. No sinking into fairy tales or parables, no princesses and dragons, magic journeys or circus clowns.'[2] The children in the plays are represented by adults: 'Characters are portrayed through how they act rather than how they are.'[3] What they do is – by implication at least – political.

> Political theatre for children? God help us! Yet anyone seriously interested in the development of children must ask themselves whether traditional children's theatre with the emphasis on mystery, mystification, the power of supernatural agencies, magic, mindless clowning, irrational fear, and personal helplessness (with all their highly reactionary political implications) is preferable to an emancipatory children's theatre which confronts, questions and challenges received social attitudes and behaviour, through comedy and song. GRIPS believes that its work can only be effective when it is entertaining, and that means working (like Molière, like Brecht, like Dario Fo, and like John McGrath with 7:84)

through comedy; not to reflect and nurture existing prejudices but to throw a critical light on social conditions.[4]

The working method of the company involves a creative interchange between author and performers. Kift has both written for them and translated their work. It was in 1979 that a GRIPS play, *Max und Milli* (*Things that go Bump in the Night*), created at the behest of the director, Volker Ludwig, was first produced in Britain. The translation was commissioned by Nick Barter at the Unicorn Theatre where it broke box-office records but attracted deplorably little critical attention.

> The theme of the play is fear; fear of the dark, fear of being bullied by other children, fear of being left alone in the house at night, fear of being hit by parents and the joy and strength of making friends and being able to conquer that fear.[5]

In 1983, another specialist children's theatre, Polka, departed from its traditional fare to the extent of producing a GRIPS play, *All in Stitches*, which had been premiered in Berlin under the title *Heile, Heile Segen* in 1980. Volker Ludwig and Christian Veit were the authors, Roy Kift the translator. This piece was also for younger children and also aimed at dispelling fear – this time of hospitals.

> Hospitals are big, strange places. They don't just frighten children. What's worse, you're feeling rotten when you go in there! This play aims to dispel some fears of hospital but also to say two things about life in general. First you can always use a new experience to

make friends, and learn to help others. Second, adults have their own fears and problems, too, even when they have children to look after.[6]

The performance of 'All in Stitches' at the Polka Children's Theatre, 21 April 1983

There was something incongruous about staging a play such as *All in Stitches* in an ornate and fanciful proscenium-arch auditorium, better attuned to leading the audience into dream-land than pouring metaphorical daylight on to secret fears. It provided the opportunity – as does the staging of Brecht's plays in the elaborate Theater am Schiffbauerdamm – to make a feature of frustrating conventional expectations. Paul Harman from Merseyside Young People's Theatre was directing and he chose an arrangement of angled flats upstage of whatever furniture was deemed necessary (two beds) to evoke a hospital ward. The audience for this morning performance consisted, at the outset, of ten young children, three woman, a babe in arms and me. The demystification started before the show with the 'nurses' sallying among the spectators taking temperatures and explaining the different grades of staff. Adult actors and actresses were to play the children in the story (and it worked perfectly), and Harman chose a coloured girl for Katherine, aged six, who was lying on a bed playing a cassette when the performance opened.

Nurse Anna came in and announced a new inmate. Very soon the inmate was heard approaching with a scream: 'I wanna go home!' Susy, the screamer, aged five, came on with her disgusted and exasperated mother. Susy had come to have her tonsils out. Nurse persuaded Mother to leave her daughter here. The Nurse admitted to the patient that the operation would 'hurt a bit'. Katherine had no paticncc with Susy and whipped up a bit of laughter at her expense. A kind doctor came in and took a blood sample from Susy. Susy was allowed by the writer to voice all her fears but the reassurance pouring in from nurse and doctor soon banished them. Katherine brought the scene to an end by kidding Susy that the anaesthetic would consist of a wooden hammer.

We moved to the next scene without taking a full blackout. It was midday next day and Susy's operation had been delayed. Katherine continued to make Susy's fears seem nonsensical by exaggerating them. In came 'good old Alfred', a male nurse, to collect the meal plates. He, too, was breezily reassuring. 'Where have you got all this nonsense about a wooden hammer?' The actor carefully took the audience in with his 'look', bathing them in reassurance too. Susy was by this time relaxed enough with Katherine to tickle her as a punishment. Alfred departed and Shocker, a patient with bandages and a leg plaster, arrived. He had a very wide mouth and a genuinely funny face. He pretended to be a doctor and to examine Katherine's stitches, but a sterner nurse, Nurse Frances, sent him out. He returned, though, and the three children played doctors and nurses in a high-spirited way. A practical joke by the girls, involving pouring water on Shocker as he came in, misfired and Susy's mother got it as she entered. She got irritated and Nurse Frances excused the hospital with a little speech about shortage of staff. Somehow the intended humour did not get the intended response from the audience.

The third scene took place at night. By this time Susy was scornful of the fuss Katherine made about her stitches hurting. Shocker and Alfred burst in and encouraged them all to make up a song called: 'In Hospital'. Again the fear was exorcised with laughter. He sang of a pair of 'itchy tonsils':

> Off they went to the doctor
> Begging for a better life.
> He said, "It's never too late to operate
> And whipped them out with a knife.
> Ow! Ow! Ow! Ow! Ow!

More high jinks with Shocker and then a quiet bit where Katherine and Susy talked of their mums and Katherine showed Susy some postcards from her dad. Katherine bid her have a nice dream about her operation and she literally did this. We saw the dream sequence on stage. To the accompaniment of percussion a comic operation was acted out in which the surgeons were Alfred, Anna and Shocker. The stage was bathed in green light and despite the daft events, there was something quite frightening about it all; the first time the audience itself was invited to feel fear. Daylight supervened and Susy was taken for her operation. Blackout.

A huge interval now occurred to 'give time to absorb and talk about' it all, but it was too long for the handful of kids. Actually a school party arrived – late!

The second half began. Susy had had her operation and was luxuriating in a continuous supply of ice-cream for her throat. Katherine persuaded her to ask for some more and pass it on to her. Nurse Frances, too, turned out to have a heart of gold. The girls swopped information about daddies. Shocker was wheeled in. He had had another accident and had broken his arm. On the other arm was a drip. Nurse Anna carefully explained it: 'This drip here feeds you liquid food and drink directly into your blood.

That way you don't get hungry and you get better quickly.' It was a tribute to the cast that the attention of the new arrivals in the audience was quickly hooked. Katherine's 'white' granny arrived. A little bit peremptory and knowing what was best for Katherine. Granny was very secretive about Daddy and there were hints of some family tragedy. However, Susy's curiosity about this was superseded when in burst a comic foreigner who turned out to be Shocker's dad. He was an emigrant from Italy, cross about the suicidal antics of his son but lovable. In his turn, he was very taken with Granny, and, on cue, on came Alfred to encourage the invention of another song, 'The Granny Song'. Nurse Frances arrived to take Katherine's stitches out and the audience dutifully laughed at the procedure. There were three and Katherine shared them with her fellow-sufferers. Her scar, displayed to Shocker, elicited the reponse: 'It ain't arf funny, your scar. All bumpy.' Night fell and it was Katherine's turn to have a nightmare. She was in distress at being deserted by her father. Her screams woke up the others, who made a fuss of her. It was less easy for the audience to empathise with Katherine's fears as the cause was not elaborated upon. Next, jokes were made about Shocker's 'death leap' that broke his arm, and then the children decided to play a trick on Granny by changing the beds over so that she thought the covered form of Shocker was Katherine. Before it happened a new patient was heard approaching, complaining loudly as Susy had done at first, and Susy, now enlightened, emancipated and thoroughly demystified, expressed her scorn: 'Cor, what a fuss about nothing!' The trick on Granny worked and it made the audience laugh aloud. Granny had come to take Katherine home. Conviviality, love and harmony reigned and a final song sturdily scoffed at fear – rejoicing in the success of treatment and recovery. As happy an ending as the most ardent of fairy-tale fans could have desired. Not inappropriate, now, to the romantic auditorium of the Polka Theatre.

All in Stitches is an example of instrumental theatre. Like *Arthur Rosebud's Revelation*, it sets out to use theatre to bring about a state of mind preconceived as being desirable. There are hints about the private lives of Katherine and Susy but the focus is on the girls as patients where they act out typical and representative roles. Apart from in the dream sequence, fear is brusquely dismissed without being evoked. The plot was liberally tricked out with comic episodes and the sort of jolly song that is a feature of the GRIPS company's house style. It shows one aspect of hospital experience as *Dead Easy* showed another. Hospital here was such a romp one could imagine the audience finding it difficult to wait before being admitted themselves. (In *Dead Easy*, the surgeon was Death!) Despite the starkness of the moralising and the thinness of the plot, the audience were absorbed in all the fun. Possibly the paucity of numbers made them feel too exposed to muck about, anyway. *All in Stitches* deals with a real social challenge which anybody might have to face, but as a play it does not invite the audience to share with it an exploration of reality. Artistic truth is harder won.

Roy Kift is probably better known for his own original play, *Stronger than Superman*, but it, too, received its first airing at GRIPS. Unlike *All in Stitches*, it has achieved the accolade of print (Amber Lane Press). It is very much like the other play, though, in style. It, too, aims at enlightenment for the prejudiced (characters and audience) and raises issues and presents information (though not so clumsily as to spoil the play). 'As with all GRIPS plays, the underlying dynamic seems to be to inculcate a progressive critical consciousness in the children of this generation, to bear fruit in the coming decade.'[7]

It is disability that this play attempts to demystify, and particularly that which results from spina bifida. The victim, this time, is Chris, aged ten. His condition 'handicaps' the lives of his sister, Paula (aged nine), and their mother. A boy, Kevin, is the first to underestimate and patronise the cripple. He has successors in officialdom. 'The whole idea of individual "strength" – doctors, security men, the cinema manager . . . the social worker, in a word, all the mini-supermen – is coming under fire.'[8]

The threat from Barraclough, the Head of the Social Services Department, who has the power to pack Chris off to a 'special school', hangs over the family for much of the play, but the 'plot' is as simple as that of *All in Stitches*. Tricks and games are played but to more serious purpose than in *All in Stitches*. Acting about, Kevin is sitting in Chris's wheelchair when Barraclough suddenly enters, mistakes Kevin for Chris and reaps embarrassment by it. The children play doctors and nurses to expose the arbitrariness of the power they wield. (One is reminded of *A Day in the Death of Joe Egg* in much of this.) Kevin learns disability from the inside when he (too conveniently?) breaks his own leg. Threats are triumphed over, though, and some of the prejudiced (Kevin and Moody, the cinema manager) reform. A major point in this play is that the handicapped are not a lower form of life.

> CHRIS: And spastics aren't stupid either! They're as bright as I am, they've just got problems talking.
> PAULA: Right! The only people who are stupid are the people like you who make stupid jokes about spastics.
>
> [Kevin stands there embarrassed for a moment]

Other features of GRIPS plays to be found in *Stronger than Superman* are songs and the use of props to explain abstruse processes in a concrete and comprehensible way. The dialogue, unfiltered by translation this time, is abrasive, snappy and funny. The victim, Chris, is not allowed to feel sorry for himself.

The genuine intelligence of spastics whose lack of physical control gives the impression that they are stupid is a theme of Chris Hawes's play, *On His Own Two Feet*, written for the Duke's Playhouse, Lancaster, in 1982. It tells the story of Kevin, a young spastic boy, from before he was even born to his acceptance for his true worth. Terry and Jean, his father and mother, occupy a more important role than the mother in Kift's play, and their marriage takes some strain. An educational psychologist recommends a day centre for Kevin, and the play charts his learning progress through learning to speak to learning to relate. The clever device of having the 'normal' side of Kevin as the narrator and commentator helps the young audience react 'normally' and without complicating embarrassment.

The performance of 'On His Own Two Feet' at Gleadless Middle School, Sheffield, by the Sheffield Crucible Vanguard Company, 1983

The acting space at Gleadless Middle School had audience on three sides, with the end section consisting of a pair of doors. The pre-show music led us into the action with the sight of Kevin, in 'spastic mode', moving to his chair. The effectiveness of this assault on the audience's sensibilities was attested by their obvious unease and uncertainty whether or not to laugh. Relief was at hand, though, as

Kevin slipped into his normality mode and introduced the play – which he claimed he had written himself.

The story began before Kevin was born. Kevin described the wooing of Mum by Dad. The scene was rather heavy-handed caricature but it was saved by brisk production. There was also a special poignancy, however, in Kevin's comment: 'In love comics, once you've married him, all your problems are over for ever and ever. In real life they're only just starting.' Terry was out a lot with a band (he being a saxophone player) and Jean wanted a child and a new home. Then Kevin started to tell the audience a joke about a 'spazzo'. The audience sniggered and giggled and it seemed to me a risky thing for Kevin to do. Jean had her wish and became pregnant and – another bold and interesting theatrical device – she spoke of her delight directly to Kevin as narrator. Kevin told another joke about 'spazzos' but I was not sure in dramatic terms why. I was uneasy about the kind of laughter I heard and I wondered if the joke was meant to serve as a kind of pre-emptive strike against the potential mockers; getting our laugh in first, so to speak. Did it take away the audience's responsibility to take the subject seriously?

The baby was born prematurely and the doctor at the hospital was very reassuring. The director contrived a highly spectacular birth scene in terms of a circus act introduced by Terry dressed as ringmaster. Jean held a hoop and Kevin somersaulted through it – to music. A taped conversation among the doctors was heard, giving the chilling news that something was wrong with the birth and there might be brain damage. Heartbeats followed and Kevin got into his wheelchair. The audience watched and listened with rivetted attention.

Kevin was taken home and a midwife paid a visit. She spotted strange symptoms in Kevin and the presence of the older Kevin made for a powerful dramatic irony from the audience's point of view. Terry (reluctant for fear of losing pay) and Jean took Kevin to a hospital for examination. The consultant woffled his explanations in medical jargon and finally came to the (devastating) point: 'Your son is a spastic.' By way of contrast, a song: 'I wanna be straight', mimed by Kevin to a guitar and Terry on the saxophone in a fantasy sequence, anaesthetised us from the pain a little. In the same sequence, Terry rejected his son and Kevin wryly commented: 'He always was a dreamer, me Dad.'

Kevin announced that he was now four years old and the next scene, with an educational psychologist, began. Terry and Jean argued whether Kevin should be sent to a special school for the physically handicapped and it was agreed that he should go to day centre. This part was narrated by the psychologist.

An early-morning scene followed, with Kevin, as spastic, being given breakfast. Passing tribute here should be paid to the brilliantly authentic acting of the man playing Kevin, as spastic. It was totally convincing and impressed the audience. What followed was more dubious, I thought. Talk turned to toilets and Kevin delivered a 'normal' racing commentary making a joke of the likelihood that Kevin would wet himself before the bus reached its destination – the 'loony school': 'The driver is being extremely co-operative and driving all over the cats' eyes and so, as I said, I think we can look forward to a really great wetting on the Loony Bus today.' In the end he *did* wet himself. Despite the popularity the actor had attracted to Kevin hitherto, this joke fell flat. Once again, it seemed as if the writer did not trust the young audience to cope with the plain truth; as if, again, he was determined to anticipate the laughter and remain in control. Actually, Kevin's pain and humiliation did, subsequently, earn their sympathy.

A school scene. Kevin's facility for slipping between 'spastic' and 'normal' modes showed us his real frustration at being able to read but not able to *show* that he could. He cashed in on his apparent incompetence in some areas to manipulate his teachers into letting him play in the sand-pit. Certainly this precluded any easy appeal to the audience on Kevin's part for sympathy. Two other children entered the play: Tracy, a likeable and considerate local girl, and Darren, a bully. Kevin wanted a normal relationship with Tracy, but was unable to express his feelings. Meanwhile, a rift was growing between his parents. Terry still wanted Kevin put away. There was another fantasy interlude with Kevin in the middle of the stage and four voices (those of Jean, Terry, Tracy and Darren) bombarding him from four sides with mockery and criticism, a successful piece of expressionism.

Kevin reconciled himself to the Residential School and played tricks on his new teacher while pretending to be backward. Terry told Jean he 'missed' Kevin and that he had been wrong to be ashamed of the boy. At school, Kevin learned to say his name and there was much encouragement and empathy among the audience. He also started to walk. Next he donned a device called a unicorn, helping him to type with his head. He typed, 'Hello, Dad', and this led into a scene with Terry. Kevin was, by now, sixteen and he could talk to people fairly freely. Dad reflected that he, too, was 'trapped' – as Kevin was in his body. 'I'm trapped in something else, I always have been. Working in that factory, earning money, finding a bit of love every now and again.' It is the 'everybody's handicapped' theme of Roy Kift's *Stronger than Superman*. Possibly, though, this is a not altogether helpful blurring of boundaries. A new rapport, however, was established between father and son. Tracy, now also grown up, reappeared and invited Kevin to a disco. A fantasy disco in which Darren (the bully) met Tracy and tried to pick her up only to be humiliated by a suave, uncrippled Kevin. A real disco sequence followed in which Tracy told Kevin (in his wheelchair) that she had asked him for himself and not out of pity: 'I didn't feel sorry for you when I asked you out . . . I don't feel sorry for you. Don't you understand?'

Final home scene. A social worker called with the news that the promised lift (to be installed in the house) would be subject to delay. It was a protracted scene of 'documentary' interest and the audience got bored and restless. Kevin, alone, changing to spastic, closed the play.

On the whole, the production was very successful. It was, as has been said, well served by a fine virtuoso performance by the actor playing Kevin, who controlled the audience's reactions to a large degree, with the useful device of the different 'modes' – spastic and normal – to demonstrate the real intelligence of the boy. Like *Stronger than Superman* it gave more weight to the boy than to the parents even if Hawes's play did involve a spectacular transformation of Dad. Early on, the means of production drew too much attention to themselves, but (as with Brenton's *The Education of Skinny Spew*) the device of allowing the boy to make knowing comments before being born made for a successful irony. Like Kift, Hawes aimed, by and large, at a humorous treatment rather than a gloomy one, but there were some uncertainties of tone. Jokes about spastics sat uneasily in the action and I think showed a lack of faith in the maturity of the young audience. It was not clear what was gained by the inclusion of the first (fantasy) disco, and the play had reached its effective end when Tracy accepted Kevin for what he was. The documentary material which followed was tedious and preachy. Earlier, too, in the scene where Kevin is in the Special School doing this training, the information content outweighed the dramatic interest.

Best of Friends, by Noel Greig, as we noted earlier, acquired notoriety by treating the explosive theme of 'gay sexuality'. I am not concerned, in the immediate context, with whether or not the play might 'promote' or incite homosexual behaviour in the young, but with the quality of the piece as a basis for artistically truthful performance. I saw it performed on two occasions by different companies and the implications for meaning of the different directorial decisions and the acting were noticeable.

The story is as follows. In 1945, a train heads for Scarborough. One of the carriages contains a young man on his own, Bernie, a woman and her husband and their red-haired daughter, Rita, and a baby. Bernie impulsively nurses the baby and earns the family's help in finding accommodation when they arrive. Bernie finds a job, too, and stays in Scarborough. Bernie has formed an attachment with Rita but she has to go home to Nottingham with the rest. Eighteen months later (1947) Bernie writes to Rita, says that he has got the promise of a council house and asks her to marry him. Bernie loses his job afterwards. They have a child, Nigel, who is brought up harshly by his dad, who wants him to grow up macho. But Nigel prefers to consort with a poor, deprived little scruff called Janet. When Nigel takes to study in a serious way, Janet loses interest in him and when the baby Bernie had nursed on the train turns up as full-grown woman, Janet takes up with her in a passionately devoted sort of way.

Nigel's mother dies of cancer. While having a nosebleed on the beach, Nigel meets a suave, middle-aged man called Carol, who photographs him and lets Nigel takes his photograph too. Carol leaves him with an invitation to come and visit. On another occasion, Nigel saves an old woman from sinking sand. Her name is Nina, an artist, who lives – with Carol! Nigel does visit Carol's house and is given the two snaphsots. Later, Nigel spots another photo in an album, a photo of Carol and another man. Fascinated, he 'borrows' it. Bernie starts to become curious about Nigel's movements and he quizzes the boy. Nigel tells him he's been seeing 'Carol' and Dad's delighted that his son is going out with a girl. Nina tells Nigel that she and Carol are not married. Nigel sees another picture of Carol, this time with a sailor friend and dancing! He becomes overwrought. Nina calls on Nigel, having learned his home address from a letter Nigel accidentally dropped at Carol's house. Nigel blurts out his conclusion that 'Carol is a queer.' Dad barges in and grabs the photo which Nigel happens to be brandishing. To Nigel's amazement and horror, Dad confesses he used to know Carol and that he was the sailor in the photo. Nigel runs away and joins the Navy and finds himself on a boat bound for the Falkland Islands. He has a letter from Janet urging him to forgive his dad. Then Nigel, too, acquires a sailor friend, David, but the boat is hit by a missile and David is killed. Nigel is injured and winds up in hospital back home. A letter from Bernie tells him that Carol has died. Bernie meets Dad at the funeral and Dad explains all, especially why he tried to bring up his son to be a man. Janet, we learn, is at Greenham Common protesting against nuclear weapons.

Looked at closely, the twists and turns of the plot are

very contrived. Coincidences abound. Father and son happen to associate with the same man; the baby in the train becomes Barbara who comes back to Scarborough and happens to be a lesbian (thus helping Janet to discover herself); the dropped letter, revealing Nigel's address to Nina; the photo which happens to find its way to Bernie; the Nigel – David relationship which neatly parallels that between Bernie and Carol. Nina happens to live with Carol but this device is useful to red-herring the audience away from Carol's sexual proclivities. There do seem to be an unconscionable number of homosexuals and lesbians around in the same place all at once. Yet despite its plea for the acceptability of homosexuals, the actual sexual element in the play is kept down, and the 'just good friends' aspect of the relationships pushed to the front. Easier for kids to handle, perhaps? The characterisation is not particularly convincing and everybody is lovable deep down. The only real conflict is between father and son, and father is allowed to over-explain at the end his earlier Freudian motivation in bullying his son.

The short-episode structure allows for fluidity of flashback. The preponderance of narrative and description, while sometimes sharp and well observed in its detail, and useful for alienating, clogs the action at times and degenerates into 'fine writing'. 'North and South go the great roads of England. From the sprawling cities of production to the sleek South and back again, tangling together in the gritty knot of the Midlands, then breaking free and springing on their way.' The respectability of homosexual relationships may be the main theme but other issues are dragged in by the scruff of the neck. The mention that Rita has cancer serves as an excuse to preach about defence spending:

> Perhaps the money spent on bombs and napalm, guns, rockets and tanks could have helped Rita, But after all, it's natural to spend half the wealth of the world on death, rather than on the means to stop it. Or so it seemed, to listen to the leaders of the nation talking from the television screen.

The historical background helped at times to motivate the plot, but the general and particular did not cohere as well as they might (contrast *Raj*, for instance). Janet ends up conveniently at Greenham Common, with the anti-nuclear protesters.

Performances of 'Best of Friends'

My first encounter with *Best of Friends* was on the evening of 19 June 1986, at Garibaldi School Youth Club, Mansfield, performed by the Perspectives Theatre Company. The setting, an abstract structure of geometric shapes which often got in the way, meant nothing to me. The audience consisted of a handful of teenagers who knew each other and who were both shocked and titillated and giggled with embarrassment. The presentation was altogether too worthy and earnest for them.

More successful, in my view, was the production by Phil Clarke with the Sheffield Crucible Vanguard Theatre at Chaucer School, Sheffield, on the evening of 5 October 1987. Carol and Bernie were played by a lively black actor. A black girl took over the part of one of the male actors, which helped as a distancing device. The audience were largely sixth fomers and the house was pretty full, thanks partly to some publicity earlier on the radio programme *You and Yours* (BBC Radio 4). The setting, unlike the stark, angular, gymnastic effort at Mansfield, was colourful and warm, all coloured lights and green waves. Where Mansfield's had been portentous, Sheffield's was hearty and comic. The black actor played Carol for the caricature he basically was. We were involved enough with Nigel to share his shock (and this could be sensed in the audience) on discovering his father was (coincidentally) a 'queer'. *Best of Friends* did not become a masterpiece in Phil Clarke's hands but it worked better the way he tackled it.

Before the infamous Clause 28 reared its ugly head, Noel Greig had been commissioned by Phil Clarke to write another play for Vanguard. Early in 1988, *Plague of Innocence* went on tour. It is set in Eyam, in Derbyshire, the famous village whose seventeenth-century residents virtually committed suicide by heeding the (well-meant) advice of the vicar, and shutting themselves off from the outside world, thereby relinguishing any chance of avoiding the plague. However Greig's play takes place at the very end of 1999. The leader of the country is the Primo and his problem is to prevent the spread of AIDS. He actually uses AIDS as an excuse to persecute homosexuals. In Orwellian fashion, he suppresses the truth. Certain words – or certain of their applications – are banned (for example 'love') while others are endorsed (for example 'Potentials'). In the end, so wide is the range of possible sources of infection (even dreams) that almost anybody can be a Potential. Compulsory testing is introduced. In fact, there is a vaccine but the authorities deny its existence. Some of the characters are engaged in smuggling it to sufferers in Eyam.

The five actors, three woman and two men, take various roles. One episode brings the subject home to school audiences. Gerald is a teacher and Winston, a pupil, falls in love with him, but that is now a situation which bristles with danger. Plot, though, in *Plague of Innocence*, far from drawing attention to itself, tends to sink out of sight. Greig uses the narrative mode widely again in this play and the actors are often required to speak in chorus, with particular effect in the promulgation of decrees. The explicitness of the commentary sometimes gives rise to special pleading, though. In this play Greig openly denies the importance of sex when measured against personal relationships ('Gay's not just sex: it's all the parts of me'), but he takes the dictator and his cronies to task for being afraid of 'bodies' and 'touching'. It is innocence that is the plague in official eyes.

Some weighty issues, here, and an open challenge, but not a lot of dramatic action. Interestingly the script was sent to the Sheffield authorities to be vetted but no objection was raised. Perhaps the Primo is still slouching towards Bethlehem to be born.

8
Postscript

The artistic achievements of theatre for the young are impressive. At best, it engages both young minds and – in different ways – adult ones. Ulterior motives (other than artistic) among its creators and practitioners, if allowed free rein, may distort the impact and impair the quality of the artefact. As an aesthetic phenomenon, YPT evinces a concern of all good art to encapsulate some truth about the world. Not 'socialist truth' or something of the kind, but the truth that does not need validation outside the living performance, the truth which wins the endorsement of our imaginations, signalling that a 'possible world' has come into being.

What distinguishes theatre for the young from theatre for adults is the self-conscious way it targets an audience which is not yet mature, to the extent, at times, of pinpointing a specific and limited age range. Michael Billington, as we saw in the first chapter, thought this was attempting not merely the impossible, but the undesirable. Children these days, so the argument goes, are exposed to the same television as adults and therefore are capable of wrestling with adults concerns. The pungent title of Neil Postman's book, *The Disappearance of Childhood*, reveals that he, too, has observed the trend. The difference is that Postman deplores it.

> We wish to keep this knowledge from children because, for all its reality, too much of it too soon is quite likely to be dangerous to the well-being of an unformed child.
>
> This is not to say that children must be protected from all forms of violence or moral degeneracy. As Bettelheim has demonstrated in *The Uses of Enchantment*, the importance of fairy tales lies in their capacity to reveal the existence of evil in a form that permits children to integrate it without trauma. This is possible not only because the content of fairy tales has grown organically over the centuries and is under the control of adults (who may, for example, modify the violence or the ending to suit the needs of a particular child) but also because the psychological context in which the tales are told is usually reassuring and is, therefore, therapeutic. But the violence that is now revealed over television is not mediated by a mother's voice, is not much modified to suit the child, is not governed by any theory of child development. It is there because television required material that comes in inexhaustible variety. It is also there because television directs everything to everyone at the same time, which is to say, television cannot keep secrets of any kind. This results in the impossibility of protecting children from the fullest and harshest disclosure of unrelenting violence.[1]

Sensitive children's theatre, too, takes account of the terms on which a young audience can cope with the darker side of life without pretending it is not there. Its very theatricality means that the child is protected from the illusion that what it is watching is 'real' life, whereas the frightening thing about television is that it seems to be 'transparent'.

The world of YPT has, to some extent, to be seen through a child's eyes. A word which recurs when talking about writing for the young is 'innocence'. It can mean lacking worldly know-how, but it can also describe a positive standpoint from which to view, to appreciate or to criticise the world of adult experience. The innocence of the child vision does not have to be located in and expressed through a child character but it can be. We may recall Peter Pan's legitimate revulsion from the bourgeois world of work, the trust (to be betrayed) that Nandita exercises, the struggle of spastic Kevin against the well-meaning but insensitive blundering of the experts or the growing resilience of twoo as he manages to outplay his mockers and follow his personal liking for Daphne.

Our brief historical survey distinguished the two main lines of development in the field of YPT, that of the entertainers and that of the educators. Applying aesthetic standards only, there was seen to be merit in both kinds of product. Nor is it a matter of fantasy versus realism. As Postman's reference to Bettelheim illustrates, fantasy can be a mode of knowing as well as an escape, and social realism can simplify and sentimentalise. A few years ago, Paul Harman, of Merseyside YPT, outraged entrenched opinion in SCYPT by suggesting that they opened their doors to companies such as 'Unicorn, Caricature and Polka and the unsubsidised ones like Seagull, West Midlands or Pumpkin'. He went on: 'To function as a united body for the benefit of all we will have to admit the validity of a broad range of aims, methods and philosophies. Not the least benefit will be the creation of a larger forum for comparison of standards and debate.'[2] Citing the example of Denmark, he wrote: 'The "left socialist" companies predominate but all recognised a current resurgence of interest in "pure entertainment", guizing, clowning etc. and non-realistic, fantasy-based plays."[3] David Wood, from the other side of the divide, also pleads for an end to the mutual antagonism: 'I still believe that it is the job of all children's theatre practitioners to push, push, push for the recognition of the work as a legitimate art form.'[4] He thinks he detects the beginnings of mutual respect:

> I believe there have been some signs of a healthy cross-fertilisation of TIE work and children's theatre work. By this I mean that some TIE teams are more aware of the need to tell a story and entertain within the structure of their programmes and on the other side of the coin, children's theatre companies are becoming aware of their responsibilities, particularly when aiming their productions at schools' audiences.[5]

Some significant changes of personnel may make for changes of policy and outlook in certain key theatres. Chris Wallis, from York YPT, had taken over from Nick Barter at the Unicorn. Vicky Ireland is moving into Richard Gill's position as Director of Polka. She has, as we saw, written plays for this theatre herself. While coming from a TIE background, she is firmly committed to the belief that fantasy is what the youngest people need. If there are changes, they seem likely to be tactfully gradual. David Holman, an institution in himself, left these shores for Australia where he engaged in showing the Australians to themselves.

Across the board, those working in theatre for the young are up against the common enemy of bankruptcy (and not just Young People's Theatre companies). The scramble is on for (often capricious) sponsorship. TIE companies worry that money might be supplied at the cost of artistic freedom. More seriously, some view with alarm the Government's education policy which is to establish a common core curriculum in secondary schools, with Drama relegated to the sidelines. Where will TIE work fit in? The new General Certificate of Secondary Education requires a large investment of time and effort on course work. 'How many teachers will be able to take on, not just the visiting theatre company, but, as is the case with Theatre Centre, teacher visits, workshops, pre-planning and the accompanying work suggested in a resourceful workpack?'[6]

Ironically the value of their work has been recognised by more institutions of higher education and professional associations. Sheffield Crucible Vanguard Company, for instance, has been invited to perform at national conferences of bodies like the National Association for the Teaching of English, and at the local university and has managed to integrate its programmes with internal courses at the Sheffield Polytechnic.

David Wood has been told by the Arts Council that he can no longer expect guaranteed future funding. Barring a miracle, this could spell the end of tours by Whirligig. He identifies a depressing new outcome of the operation of market forces, another threat to genuine creativity and originality:

> One of the developments of the past few years has been the growing number of successful commercial tours of children's plays to the big theatres. I view this with

> considerable suspicion! One or two companies are very sincere in their aims, but others simply see a commercial opportunity. Usually they find a very strong title, adapt the book or television series into a play, and throw it on rather cheaply, not spending too much time or attention on sets and costumes, employing fairly inexperienced actors, making a bit of money, then dropping out of the game. In other words they don't show much commitment to children's work as a whole, simply to one project which looks like being a commercial success . . . . My concern is that these productions will squeeze out major children's theatre productions from companies (like Whirligig!) which need subsidy to achieve the standards they legitimately aim for.[7]

On the other hand, he finds a cause for mild rejoicing:

> I think the attitudes of many theatre managers have improved. Maybe they are getting younger! Many of them possibly have children. Children as an audience are not quite so reluctantly thought of as part of many theatre programmes, both subsidised and commercial.[8]

Wood admits, however, that there is no simple equation linking amount of money with artistic quality:

> The fact is that everybody is underfunded and there is a bottomless pit! In many ways it would be wrong if that pit were ever filled. We need something to fight against.[9]

It is true that dependence on commercial sponsorship has adversely affected the quality of much American Children's Theatre but, on the other hand, the bounty of state subsidies in countries like the Soviet Union and the German Democratic Republic has induced complacency and conservatism, rootedness in the personnel and overmanning.

In describing in detail a representative range of plays in performance I have tried to identify the variety of other factors, too, which contribute to their success or failure. I feel I can speak with conviction only of performances I was able to get to myself. Inevitably I have recorded examples of poor work from companies which normally do much better. Inevitably I have omitted to make reference to other companies which have produced work of a high standard. Sometimes plays which did not get published and existed only in the fleeting hours of a 'run' made an impact that was well worth registering.

Any play, as I have said earlier, intended for the theatre, needs assessing in the context of a stage realisation. Children's literature can more easily be a private experience. There may, of course, be adults reading to the youngsters or with them (as Postman points out). But in the theatre, the 'play' may be created by a syndicate and will certainly be mediated by theatre personnel and by other members of the audience, adult or child. We have seen how adults can preserve stale and artistically alien conventions in a way that adversely affects the seriousness of the piece. It has been argued by some that the ideal set-up would be a performance to which only children were admitted. This would, of course, presuppose a high degree of trust such as adults – even on the 'home' ground of a school – are not too ready to accord. More feasible, perhaps, would be an audience in which adults were prepared to let the children – within civilised limits – enjoy their spontaneous interplay with what is going on before them, unchivvied, unprompted and uncensored. The adults might find things they can genuinely share with the youngsters and things that appeal to them as adults, too.

Notes

1. Definitions and Principles

1. *SCYPT: A Special Statement for Delegates Attending the Arts Council of Great Britain Conference: Theatre in Education* (1984).
2. John Russell Brown, *Effective Theatre* (London: Heinemann, 1986) p. 79.
3. As argued in R. G. Collingwood, *The Principles of Art* (London: Oxford University Press, 1958) p. 152.
4. Martin Esslin, *An Anatomy of Drama* (London: Abacus, 1978) p. 109.
5. Ibid., p. 111.
6. Moses Goldberg, *Children's Theatre: A Philosophy and a Method* (Prentice-Hall, 1974) pp. 80–84.
7. Janice Jarvis and Roger Chamberlain, 'Acting in Theatre in Education', *SCYPT Journal*, vol. 11, pp. 14–25.

8. See *The Drama Advisory Panel's Children's Theatre Working Party Report* (February 1977–November 1978) Section 5.
9. Michael Billington, in the *Guardian*, 3 December 1982.
10. David Wood, 'Professional Theatre for Children – a Poor Relation?', *London Drama*, vol. 5, no. 8, pp. 8–9.
11. Collingwood, *Principles of Art*, p. 78.
12. Gavin Bolton in *Learning Through Theatre*, ed. Tony Jackson (Manchester: Manchester University Press, 1980) p. 77.
13. Ibid.
14. Eric Bentley, *The Theatre of Commitment* (London: Methuen, 1954) p. 213.
15. Collingwood, *Principles of Art*, p. 279.
16. Roy Kift, 'Getting to GRIPS with Children's Theatre', *Theatre Quarterly*, vol. x, no. 39, p. 70.
17. John Arden, 'On Comedy', *Encore*, September–October 1965, p. 16.
18. Collingwood, *Principles of Art*, p. 280.
19. Tony Jackson (ed.), *Learning Through Theatre*, p. 22.
20. Joan Aiken, *The Way to Write for Children* (London: Elm Tree Books, 1982) p. 19.
21. Peter Coveney, *The Image of Childhood* (Harmondsworth: Penguin Books, 1967) p. 32.

2. History and Evolution

1. Aidan Chambers, *Plays for Young People to Read and Perform* (London: Signal, 1982) p. 3ff.

2. John O'Toole, *Theatre in Education* (London: Hodder and Stoughton, 1976) p. 13.
3. Cora Williams, Bolton TIE, quoted in O'Toole, *Theatre in Education*, p. 14.
4. Ibid., p. 88.
5. Ibid., p. 113.
6. Christine Redington, *Can Theatre Teach?* (Oxford Pergamon, 1983) p. 94.
7. Tony Jackson (ed.), *Learning Through Theatre* (Manchester: Manchester University Press, 1980) p. 17.
8. See Redington, *Can Theatre Teach*? For this and certain other historical information, I am much indebted to this author.
9. Jackson (ed.), *Learning Through Theatre*, Introduction, p. xiii.
10. Arts Council of Great Britain, *A Policy for Theatre for Young People* (1986).

3. The Present Scene

1. Arts Council of Great Britain, *A Policy for Theatre for Young People* (1986).
2. Norman Tebbit, quoted in *The Journal* (Newcastle upon Tyne) 28 March 1983.
3. Christine Redington, *Can Theatre Teach*? (Oxford: Pergamon, 1983) p. 104.
4. Merseyside YPT brochure (1983).
5. Richard Gill, *The Story of Polka* (rev. ed, 1983)
6. Ibid.
7. Richard Gill, 'The Enchanted Theatre', *London Drama*, vol. 6, no. 2, pp. 12–13.
8. *Observer Magazine*, 25 February 1978.

4. Fantasy in a Traditional Mould

1. Peter Coveney, *The Image of Childhood* (Harmondsworth: Penguin, 1967) p. 251
2. Irene McManus in the *Guardian*, 20 December 1982.
3. Trevor Nunn in *The Times Educational Supplement*, 10 December 1982.
4. Michael Billington in the *Guardian*, 18 December 1982.
5. Robert Cushman in the *Observer*, 19 December 1982.
6. Heather Neill in *The Times Educational Supplement*, 1983.
7. Cushman, *Observer*.
8. Ibid.
9. Brian Way, Introduction to *Pinocchio* (Dobson, 1954) p. 8.
10. Aidan Chambers, *Plays for Young People to Read and Perform* (London: Signal, 1982) p. 65.
11. Brian Way, *Development Through Drama* (London: Longmans, 1967) p. 219.
12. Way, Introduction to *Pinocchio*, p. 8.
13. Chambers, *Plays for Young People*, p. 60.
14. David Wood, letter to Jeff Mercer, 19 March 1984.
15. Ibid.
16. Keith Nurse in the *Daily Telegraph*, 17 November 1983.
17. Carol Wilks in the *Guardian*.
18. Joyce McMillan in the *Guardian*, 20 December 1985.
19. Cordelia Oliver in the *Guardian*.
20. Joyce McMillan in the *Guardian*, 20 December 1985.
21. Joyce McMillan in the *Guardian*, 21 December 1984.
22. Joyce McMillan in the *Guardian*, 12 December 1986.
23. Ibid.

24. John Holt, *How Children Fail* (Harmondsworth: Penguin, 1969) p. 139.
25. Jack Cross in the *Guardian*, 20 September 1983.
26. Ibid.
27. Hazel Wilkinson in the *Guardian*, 4 October 1983.
28. Pat Friday in the *Guardian*, 25 October 1983.

5. New Fantasy

1. Rosalind Asquith, 'Children's Theatre', in *Dreams and Deconstructions*, ed. Sandy Craig (Amber Lane Press, 1980) p. 89.
2. Ibid., p. 90.
3. The *Guardian*, 6 October 1987.
4. Ibid.
5. Asquith, *Dreams and Deconstructions*, p. 88.
6. Aidan Chambers, *Plays for Young People to Read and Perform* (London: Signal 1982) p. 22.
7. Asquith, *Dreams and Deconstructions*, p. 33.
8. Chambers, *Plays for Young People*, p. 34.
9. Ibid., p. 24.

6. 'Social Realism' and Plays Based on Political Issues

1. See *SCYPT Journal*, vol. 10.
2. Les Smith in *Stage by Stage*, published by West Midlands Arts (1983/4) p. 5.
3. Pam Schweitzer, *Theatre in Education* (London: Methuen, 1980) p. 9.
4. Paul Swift, interviewed by Geoff Gillham in *SCYPT Journal*, vol. 10, p. 15.

5. *Raj* (London: Amber Lane Press, 1984) p. 63.
6. Ibid.
7. John Arden, 'On Comedy', in *Encore*, September/October 1965, p. 16.
8. Wyllie Longmore, *SCYPT Journal*, vol. 10, p. 17.
9. David Holman, *SCYPT Journal*, vol. 7, p. 35.
10. Ibid.
11. Joyce McMillan in the *Guardian*, 20 February 1987.
12. Ibid.
13. Holman, *SCYPT Journal*, vol. 7, p. 32.

7. 'Social Realism' and Plays Based on other Issues

1. Eric Bentley, *Theatre of Commitment* (London: Methuen, 1954) p. 224.
2. Roy Kift, 'Getting to GRIPS with Children's Theatre', in *Theatre Quarterly*, vol. 10, no. 39, p. 63.
3. Ibid.
4. Ibid., p. 64.
5. Ibid., pp. 67–8.
6. Programme note.
7. Roy Kift, 'A GRIPS Casebook', in *Theatre Quarterly*, vol. 10, no. 39, p. 73
8. Ibid.

8. Postscript

1. Neil Postman, *The Disappearance of Childhood* (London: W. H. Allen, 1982) pp. 93–4.
2. *SCYPT Journal*, vol. 10, p. 19.
3. Ibid., p. 21.
4. David Wood, letter to Alan England, 12 July 1988.

5. Ibid.
6. Tricia Lomax, 'The Two Jerusalems', in *SCYPT Journal*, vol. 18, p. 3.
7. Wood, letter to Alan England.
8. Ibid.
9. Ibid.

Index